SCHOLASTIC

W9-BJN-545

TEACHING READING
Differentiated Instruction With Leveled Graphic Organizers

by NANCY L. WITHERELL & MARY C. McMACKIN

NEW YORK · TORONTO · LONDON · AUCKLAND · SYDNEY
MEXICO CITY · NEW DELHI · HONG KONG · BUENOS AIRES

Teaching Resources

This book is dedicated to what began as our "writing group" and evolved
into a lifetime of fun and friendship. To our terrific friends and support group:
Jeri Gillin, Joyce Green, and Denise Marchionda.

We all need a place where we can be who we are.

Thank you for being that place.

Editor: Sarah Longhi
Cover design by Maria Lilja
Interior design by Sydney Wright
ISBN-13 978-0-545-05902-2
ISBN-10 0-545-05902-X

3 4 5 6 7 8 9 10   40   15 14 13 12 11

Contents

Introduction

Imagine that you've just walked into a first-grade classroom and are watching the teacher, who has the children's rapt attention as he finishes reading a picture book to the class. Once he finishes reading, he transitions into a lesson on story grammar. The students have already learned the concepts of character, setting, and plot. They are now learning how these elements fit together to create a story. The children excitedly recount the elements of the story while the teacher records and labels their responses on chart paper. At the end of the lesson, when the students are ready to work independently, their teacher passes out story-mapping graphic organizers as a follow-up assignment. Observing the students working independently, you realize that the story maps the students are completing are not the same. Taking a closer look, you notice slight differences, although the basic assignment seems to be the same. You have just walked into a classroom that uses leveled graphic organizers to differentiate student learning.

Differentiated Instruction

Tomlinson (1999) explains that teachers can modify three aspects of teaching: *content*, *process*, and *product*. When we differentiate by using leveled graphic organizers, we are modifying products.

We know that when we introduce a skill to a whole class (or even a subset of a class), the children in the group are not likely to learn at the same rate. Some will catch on to the skill faster than others, and some will be able to demonstrate their understanding in more complex ways than others. In order for all children to learn at an optimal pace, we must match children with a reinforcing activity that allows each one to be successful at a cognitively appropriate level. A teacher, for example, could provide whole-class instruction on character development, teaching students that a character's physical appearance, actions, and personality contribute to his or her development. After modeling how to identify and label character features, the teacher could have several students work on a graphic organizer in which they draw and write about a character's "outside" appearance and actions. Meanwhile, several other students might work on a graphic organizer that asks them to draw and write about the character's physical description and actions, and also what the character is thinking. Students might need to explain what all the features tell us about this character. Finally, the remaining students in the group would work on a graphic organizer in which they consider more deeply the "inside" and "outside" features of a character. (You can find leveled examples on pages 46–48.)

At all three levels, students are using the graphic organizers to reinforce the skill of character development that their teacher introduced to the entire group. Each student should feel successful because he or she was matched to a graphic organizer that was just right for him or her—one that was neither too easy nor too difficult.

Why Use Tiered Graphic Organizers?

In order to meet the diverse needs of students in today's classrooms, teachers must be able to design lessons that (1) meet individual instructional requirements, (2) stay within what is often mandated curriculum, and (3) ensure consistent outcomes for all students.

Time constraints place limits on the amount of individual instruction we can provide. In *Teaching Reading: Differentiated Instruction With Leveled Graphic Organizers*, we structure each whole-class mini-lesson around one central objective and then modify the follow-up activities—or student products—to meet student needs. First we teach a concept or skill to the entire class, and then we match students with graphic organizers that are "just right" for their developmental level.

When we "tier" the graphic organizers, we create planners on three levels: a *beginning* level, where students demonstrate a basic understanding of the target concept using pictures and a limited amount of writing; a *developing* level that is applicable for students who are ready to engage, with some support, in higher levels of thinking and writing than students using the beginning level organizers; and an *extending* level that is appropriate for students who are able to work, with limited support, on material that is more cognitively advanced than that of the lower two levels. Leveled graphic organizers make it possible for teachers to match each student with developmentally appropriate comprehension activities.

Although the leveled graphic organizers represent different degrees of complexity, we've designed each organizer in a set to look equally demanding and appealing. It's also important to note that graphic organizers are not end products; rather, they are planners that students use to record ideas for a subsequent activity. In the primary grades, students might work on individual organizers and then share their ideas orally in a whole-class discussion. Other times, students might use the organizers as planning tools for writing activities. In all cases, the organizers should be viewed as a means to an end, not a final product.

Building Concepts for Primary Students

A few years ago, we wrote *Teaching Reading Through Differentiated Instruction With Leveled Graphic Organizers* (Grades 4–8) (2002) and since then, a large number of primary-grade teachers have said to us, "We want leveled graphic organizers, too." And now they have them in this book, which addresses the developmental needs and interests of primary-grade children and emphasizes the need to build (as opposed to reinforce) concepts. Building a thorough understanding of literary concepts in the primary grades is crucial because these understandings form a foundation for a deeper development of these same concepts in the intermediate grades and beyond. Most students in the primary grades, for example, are probably just learning to summarize. They are learning both the term itself and the abstract idea that the word *summarize* represents. We introduce this complex concept and 14 others in this book. We begin with concrete examples and gradually move to abstract representations as we introduce each concept. It is important to note, too, that we include 15 reading skills and objectives that have been identified as important components of comprehension by researchers (Allington, 2001; Harvey & Goudvis, 2000; Keene & Zimmerman, 1997; Miller, 2002; Pinnell & Scharer, 2003; Snow, Burns, & Griffin, 1998) and through our own classroom experiences.

Techniques offered in this book to build comprehension should not be taught in isolation or in the language arts block alone, but connected in practical ways to the entire curriculum. For instance, when the class is waiting in the auditorium for a program to begin, you can keep students focused by asking them to give you words that describe the auditorium, thereby reinforcing the concept of setting. If the program is a play, afterward you can lead a discussion about the characters, the setting, and the plot of the play and then reinforce these concepts with the story map organizer. Most primary-age students need time and reinforcement to gain conceptual understandings.

How Is This Book Organized?

One of the major goals of this book is to help students become effective, independent readers. Towards this end, we incorporate in each chapter the following components from Duke and Pearson's (2002) comprehension model:

1. An explicit description of the strategy as well as when and how it should be used

2. Teacher and/or student modeling of the strategy in action

3. Collaborative use of the strategy in action

4. Guided practice using the strategy with gradual release of responsibility

5. Independent use of the strategy

You'll notice, too, that each chapter contains the same organizational structure:

❀ Names and defines a target skill

❀ Provides an activity to use with students through which we introduce the skill and related concept

❀ Transitions from a concrete activity to a piece of quality literature in order to illustrate the concept in a more abstract form

❀ Offers a model lesson in which we provide direct instruction using the skill and prepare students for the tiered graphic organizers

❀ Includes three tiered graphic organizers: Beginning, Developing, and Extended

❀ Lists two or more picture books and one chapter book, with annotations, that teachers can use in follow-up lessons

Although we present the concepts individually, we urge teachers to model a flexible,

multi-strategy approach to constructing meaning from texts.

We created the chapters in *Teaching Reading: Differentiated Instruction With Leveled Graphic Organizers* so they can be used as stand-alone chapters, to be used in any order that meets your needs and those of your students. The chapters can also be introduced as units of study that build on one another. For example, it might make sense to introduce the chapters on setting, character, and plot before you teach story mapping. In addition, the lessons and activities in this book can easily be incorporated into guided reading classrooms, used in conjunction with basal reading series, or used to reinforce concepts taught within literature circles.

Is This a Workbook?

No. This is not a reading workbook, even though some workbooks can be useful for some students. Workbooks are texts that can be used one time—once the answers have been recorded on a page, the workbook has served its purpose. Conversely, the activities in this book are open-ended and may be used over and over again as your students grow and develop.

◆ ◆ ◆

Effective teachers always strive to meet the needs of every student with whom they work. Leveled graphic organizers can assist in this process. Just imagine the possibilities they can afford your students.

Connections: Text to Self

Skill: *Evoke personal connections to literature.*

Description

Keene and Zimmerman (1997) in *Mosaic of Thought* discuss the effectiveness of encouraging students to make connections with the text they are reading. These connections are divided into three categories: connections to self, other text, and the world. To build this important concept for primary-grade children we decided to teach each concept independent of the others, although students may not always make connections that way. We begin with making connections to oneself because students naturally connect story characters and events to their own lives. For instance, losing teeth and other childhood events highlighted in picture books seem to instantly spark personal stories for most children. These memories—their personal connections—deepen children's interest in the story, their motivation to read, and their comprehension.

Getting to Know the Concept

Sharing with students how the stories you read together relate to your own life is the best way for students to understand this concept. To make these connections as real as possible for the students, begin by discussing an ordinary event that happened to you recently. For instance, last night you were having a drink of juice and stained your shirt or blouse; you were almost late to school because you couldn't find your keys; you went grocery shopping and realized you left your wallet at home. Most likely, before you even ask if something like this has happened to them, your students will be regaling you with similar stories. Explain to students that in the same way that we make connections to real-life stories, we also make connections to events that happen in books. To prepare them for a deeper understanding of characters' motives and feelings, ask them how they felt or behaved during the events they describe.

Teaching the Concept With Literature

The next step is to begin making students aware that these same types of connections can be made when they read. As we help children engage with literature, we want to enhance their understanding by encouraging them to connect to the actions, emotions, or even the goals of the characters in stories. When children are first learning to make connections to self, select books that are about events that are likely to happen in their own lives.

Model Lesson

Choose a book with a protagonist and events students can really relate to, such as *Alexander and the Terrible, Horrible, No Good, Very Bad Day* (Viorst, 1972). Children sympathize with Alexander as he encounters such things as gum in his hair, a wet sweater, siblings getting prizes, sitting in the middle, and getting in trouble at school.

Prior to reading this story to the class, tell students that you are going to share some connections to your own life as you read the story. Explain that when you make connections to the story it is just like when they made connections to the events you shared from your own life. Tell them to listen carefully to the story, as you will be asking if they have any connections to share. Begin reading and when you find a connection, such as having had gum in your hair, share the connection with your students. Then encourage them to share a similar event in their lives. Ask how they felt when they

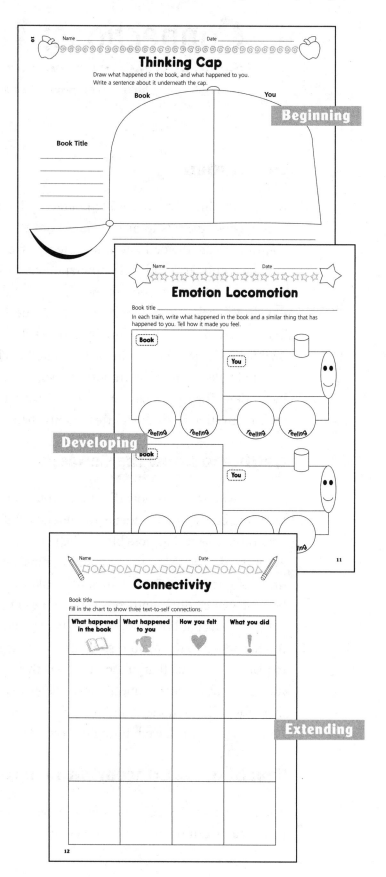

were in this situation, and what they did. Linking the story event to a real-life emotion or action leads them to a deeper understanding of the characters in the story. Continue making your own connections and soliciting them from your students as you read the rest of the book.

For additional practice, have each student complete an organizer at his or her skill level.

Graphic Organizers

Beginning: **Thinking Cap** (page 10)
Students make a connection between one or two events in the book and something they have done or something that has happened to them. For each situation, they draw what happened in the book and what happened in their own lives and then write a sentence describing these events.

Developing: **Emotion Locomotion** (page 11)
Students list two events from the book, name the corresponding events in their own lives, and describe how these situations made them feel.

Extending: **Connectivity** (page 12)
Students list three events from the book and make connections to their lives, telling how they felt and what they did in response to the situation.

Great Books for This Activity

Picture Books

Greene, R. G. (2004). *This is the teacher.* New York: Scholastic. This book is full of school experiences students can relate to.

Mayer, M. (1983). *Just go to bed.* Racine, WI: Western Publishing Company. This humorous book will have students relating to their own bedtime events.

Viorst, J. (1972). *Alexander and the terrible, horrible, no good, very bad day.* New York: Atheneum.

Chapter Book

Blume, J. (1981). *The one in the middle is the green kangaroo.* New York: Bantam-Double Day. This book is about a child who is always in the middle, yet never the center of attention.

Name _____

Date _____

Thinking Cap

Draw what happened in the book, and what happened to you.
Write a sentence about it underneath the cap.

You

Book

Book Title

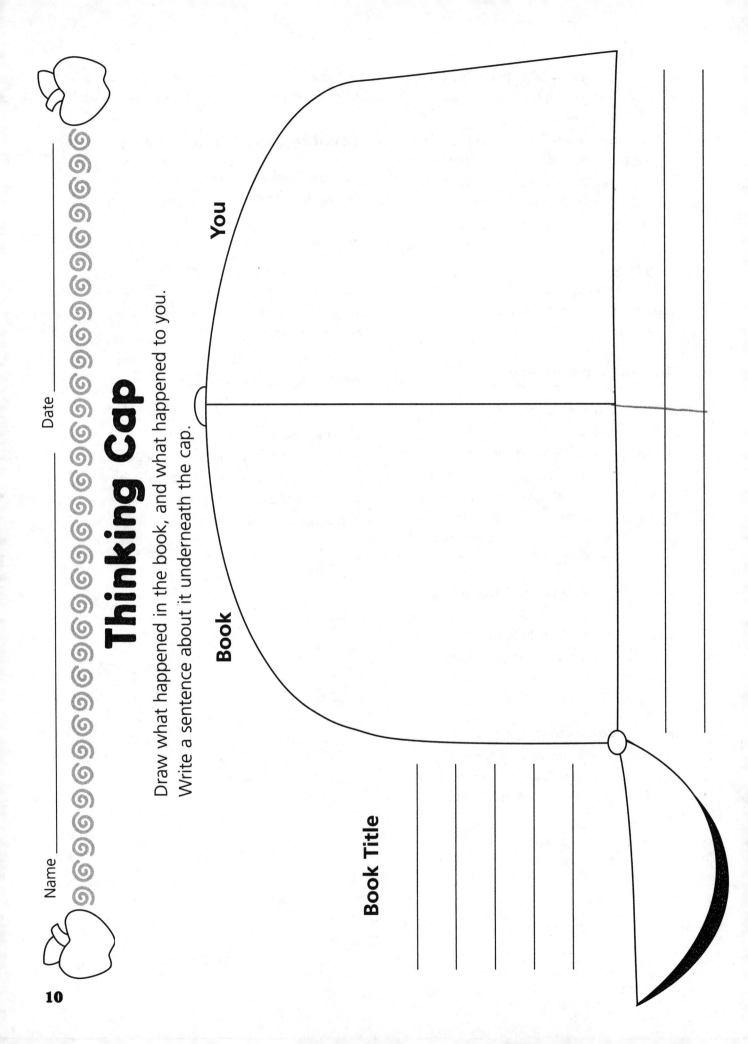

Name _____ Date _____

Emotion Locomotion

Book title _____

In each train, write what happened in the book and a similar thing that has happened to you. Tell how it made you feel.

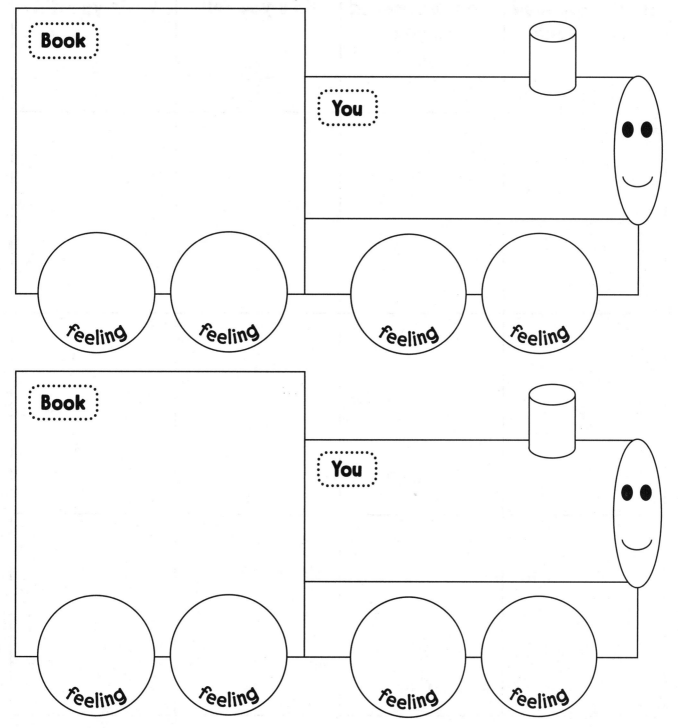

Connectivity

Book title _____

Fill in the chart to show three text-to-self connections.

What happened in the book	What happened to you	How you felt	What you did

Connections: Text to Text

Skill: *Identify text-to-text connections.*

(This lesson should follow the previous lesson on text-to-self connections.)

Description

Another type of connection Keene and Zimmerman (1997) show to be helpful for readers is one that exists between texts. In a text-to-text connection a reader makes a connection between an event in one book and an event in another. Several ways to support text-to-text connections include author studies (allowing students to compare plot and other elements of stories by the same author), book-series studies (allowing students to make connections between books that have the same characters or topics), and retelling comparisons, in which students can compare elements of well-known stories. The catalyst for a text-to-text connection may be characters' actions, motives, or feelings, or the setting or events. The connection can also be a similarity in plot. For example, using a Venn Diagram to compare one version of Cinderella with another fosters text-to-text connections as students discuss and discover how one version is like and different from the other. It is surprisingly easy for young children to make text-to-text connections, a skill you can reinforce during read-alouds, noting a similarity between the book read yesterday and the one being read today.

Getting to Know the Concept

In order to ensure that students understand the concept of text-to-text connections, be explicit in explaining that you are making connections between one text and another, and initially write these connections on a class chart. To teach the basic concept, talk about cartoon characters that students are familiar with and relate them to each other. Compare Curious George (the Saturday morning cartoon) with Sponge Bob Square Pants, or Care Bears with Strawberry Shortcake. As you talk about events, students will probably bring in other cartoon characters and events with which they are familiar, such as Mickey Mouse, Superheroes, and Ninja Turtles.

Teaching the Concept With Literature

Explain to students that just as they can compare and make connections between one cartoon or cartoon character and another, we often do the same thing with books and book characters, and that is what you will be practicing. Talk about two books you have read in class—for instance, *Miss Rumphius* by Barbara Cooney (1982) and *Mrs. Rose's Garden* by Elaine Greenstein (1996). Explain how you made connections between the two books as you read. Then begin to list the connections and allow students to chime in. Your list might include the following:

❋ Both main characters are women.

❋ Both liked to plant—Miss Rumphius planted lupines and Mrs. Rose planted vegetables.

❋ Both wanted to do something nice— Miss Rumphius wanted to leave the world a better place and Mrs. Rose wanted to get all her friends a prize.

Model Lesson

Use three simple books to begin this process, such as *Clifford's First Snow Day* (Bridwell, 1998), *The Snowy Day* (Keats, 1962), and "Down the Hill," in *Frog and Toad All Year* (Lobel, 1976). These texts contain activities to which most children can relate. If you're using these books, begin by reading *The Snowy Day*, as this book will be used as the main text in making connections. Discuss text-to-text connections as you read. Then as you read *Clifford's First Snowy Day*, tell students that this book reminds you of the book *The Snowy Day* and the Frog and Toad

story "Down the Hill," and that you will read these books to the class also. Begin with either book, and as you read, chart the text-to-text connections and add the element described in the connection—setting, events, and so on. Explain to students that you are charting text-to-text connections to show your thinking. After charting two or three connections, invite children to share their thoughts when they connect items from the two books to *The Snowy Day*. Your completed chart may look something like the one below.

Tell children that as they read a book, it's helpful to think of connections to other books because comparing books helps a reader understand characters and events better—we notice how they are the same and different. Explain that when we make text-to-text connections, we not only make connections to other books, but we can also make connections to something we read in newspapers or magazines.

For additional practice, have each student complete an organizer at his or her skill level.

Graphic Organizers

As you begin using text-to-text graphic organizers, in the beginning it may help some

The Snowy Day	Connection	Category
Snow all over----------------------------->	Clifford had snow all over	setting
Peter wanted to play in the snow---->	That's what Frog wanted to do	feelings
Peter put on a snowsuit---------------->	Frog had to dress Toad	actions
Peter's feet sank into the snow-------->	Emily's did too	actions
Peter made a snowman---------------->	Emily and Tim made one too	event
Peter slid in his snowsuit--------------->	Clifford slid in a boot	event
Peter went in the warm house------->	Emily, Clifford and Toad did too	event

students to make connections between their current book and a familiar class read-aloud.

Beginning: **Clicking With Text Connections** (page 16)

Students describe with a picture and words one text-to-text connection they made.

Developing: **Book Bonding** (page 17)

Students draw two text-to-text connections and identify the type of text-to-text connection as either character, setting, or event.

Extending: **Chart Connections: Text-to-Text** (page 18)

Students describe three text-to-text connections, list the books in which the connections are made, and identify the type of connection: setting, character, action, feeling, plot, event, and so on.

Great Books for This Activity

Picture Books

Bridwell, N. (1998). *Clifford's Snow Days.* New York: Scholastic.

Cooney, B. (1982). *Miss Rumphius.* New York: Viking Penguin.

Greenstein, E. (1996). *Mrs. Rose's garden.* New York: Simon and Schuster.

Keats, Ezra. (1962). *The snowy day.* New York: Viking.

Pinkwater, D. (1999). *Ice cream Larry.* Tarrytown, NY: Marshall Cavendish. Larry, a polar bear, has a feast in an ice cream shop's freezer.

Rey, M., Rey, H. A. (1989). *Curious George goes to an ice cream shop.* New York: Houghton Mifflin. Curious George gets into a lot of ice cream trouble!

Chapter Book

Lobel, A. (1976). *Frog and Toad all year.* New York: Harper & Row.

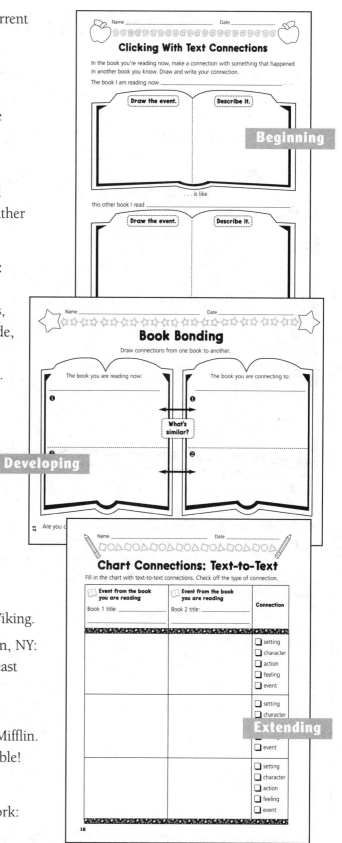

Name _____ Date _____

Clicking With Text Connections

In the book you're reading now, make a connection with something that happened in another book you know. Draw and write your connection.

The book I am reading now _____ . . .

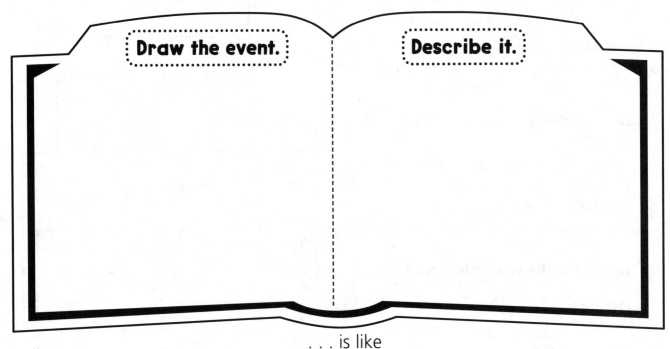

Draw the event.   Describe it.

. . . is like

this other book I read _____ .

Draw the event.   Describe it.

Name _____

Date _____

Book Bonding

Draw connections from one book to another.

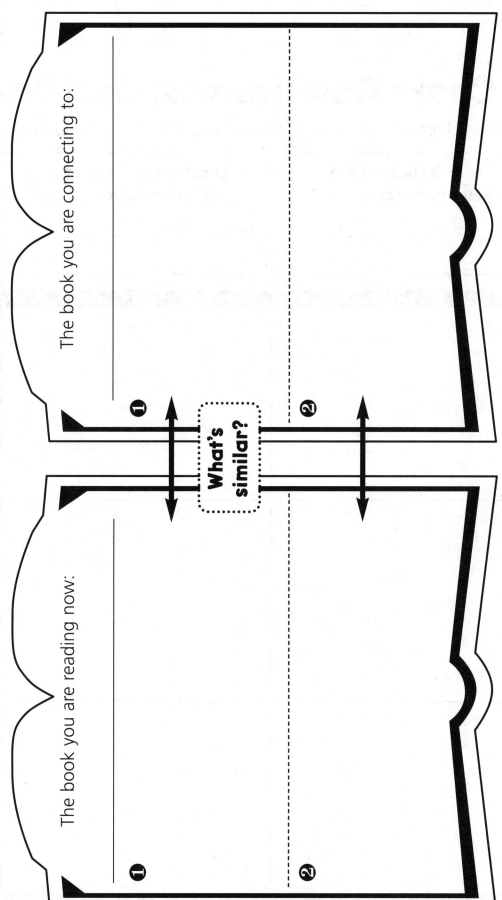

The book you are connecting to:

①
②

What's similar?

The book you are reading now:

①
②

Are you connecting the setting, the characters, or the events?

Chart Connections: Text-to-Text

Fill in the chart with text-to-text connections. Check off the type of connection.

📖 **Event from the book you are reading** Book 1 title: _____ _____	📖 **Event from the book you are reading** Book 2 title: _____ _____	**Connection**
		☐ setting ☐ character ☐ action ☐ feeling ☐ event
		☐ setting ☐ character ☐ action ☐ feeling ☐ event
		☐ setting ☐ character ☐ action ☐ feeling ☐ event

Connections: Text to World

Skill: *Identify text-to-world connections.*

(This lesson should follow the previous lessons on text-to-self and text-to-text connections.)

Description

The world is a big place, but it's much smaller to young children whose "world" often encompasses only family, school, organized sports, and perhaps religious institutions. It is the responsibility of educators to enlarge that world and help children to see circumstances through a wider lens. When reading about characters, settings, and events in books, we can help children see connections to the broader world and deepen their comprehension. In making text-to-world connections, children find similarities between elements in a book and those in the world beyond their personal experiences or their reading. These connections may come from information children have learned from family "stories," television programs, outside events they have witnessed, field trips, sports events, or museum visits. In some cases a text-to-world connection may be associated with a text-to-text connection; for example, a child might mention having read about a world event in a newspaper, online, or in a *Weekly Reader*.

Getting to Know the Concept

Once children understand text-to-self and text-to-text connections, making the transition to text-to-world will not be difficult. They need to understand the category of text-to-world as it compares to text-to-self and text-to-text. To help scaffold their understanding, draw a chart on the board that says: "Connections: Text to Self, Text to Text, Text to World." Have students define in their own words what it means to make a text-to-self connection. Write the definition on the chart, and ask for examples. Then have students define in their own words a text-to-text connection. Write the definition on the chart, and ask for examples. Now define what it means to make a text-to-world connection, and give some examples, such as the following: You're reading a book about lots of snow, and the news says it is snowing in New England; the book you're reading is about a boy getting lost in the woods, and last year a young girl did get lost in the woods and was later found; you're reading a book about a carnival, and the carnival is coming to town next week.

Teaching the Concept With Literature

Talk with students about some of the books you have been reading in class and ask what text-to-world connections they can make with these books. For instance, in *Duck for President* (Cronin, 2004), Duck engages in a number of campaigns—first he runs for "farmer," then for governor, and finally for president. Invite students to make a text-to-world connection between this storyline and what they have heard about real elections. For instance, students will be able to make text-to-world connections when Duck rides in parades, gives speeches, and goes on late-night television. They may also bring in text-to-world connections focusing on voting, and campaigning in general.

Model Lesson

In this lesson, explain to students that you are deliberately trying to make as many text-to-world connections as possible to help them understand how a book can help us think about the world, and how this connection deepens our comprehension of the book. Tell students that you are going to read *A Chair for My Mother* (Williams, 1982) and that you will stop and write down your world connection and ask if anyone else has one. Tell students that as a review, you will eventually be asking for text-to-self and text-to-text connections also. Read the book aloud and chart only the text-to-world connections. Your chart may look something like the one below.

For additional practice, have each student complete an organizer at his or her skill level.

Graphic Organizers

Beginning: **Connections: What in the World?** (page 22)
Students make one text-to-world connection by drawing and writing about the text and some aspect in the real world.

What Happens in the Book	Teacher's Text-to-World Connections	Students' Text-to-World Connections
Mother is a waitress and Josephine gets to wash salt and pepper shakers.	Salt and pepper shakers are usually on the table at restaurants.	McDonalds has little packets.
The family saves money in a jar.	Banks are for saving money.	First Bank is a bank in town.
The family is going to buy a chair.	Bob's Furniture has lots of nice chairs for sale.	They sell chairs at the flea market that are cheap.
The apartment house burned down.	There was a big fire last year and three families lost their homes.	The fire trucks came to the house next door, but didn't have to use the hose.

Developing: **Connections: Worldly Wise**
(page 23)
Students make two text-to-world connections, then write about each one and explain the connection.

Extending: **Connections: On Top of the World** (page 24)
Students write what happened in the text, then make and identify three connections, two of which must be text to world. The other one may be text to world, text to self or text to text. They will then explain what made them think of the connection.

Great Books for This Activity

Picture Books

Cronin, D. (2004). *Duck for president.* New York: Simon and Schuster.

Maccorone, G. (1994). *Soccer game.* New York: Scholastic. This simple book allows students to make connections to soccer in the news and in their community.

Madrigal, A. H. (1999). *Erandi's braids.* New York: Joanna Cotler. In this book a young Mexican girl cuts her hair to help with expenses.

Williams, V. (1982). *A chair for my mother.* New York: Greenwillow.

Chapter Book

MacLachlan, P. (1985). *Sarah, plain and tall.* New York: Scholastic. This book has a number of possible world connections, such as advertisements, storm news, and museum visits.

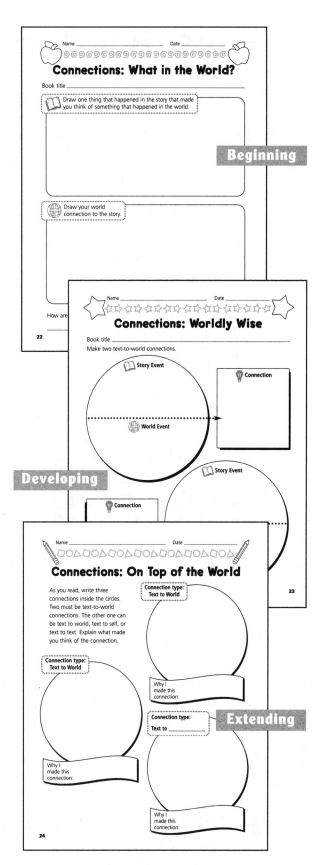

Name _____   Date _____

Connections: What in the World?

Book title _____

> Draw one thing that happened in the story that made you think of something that happened in the world.

> Draw your world connection to the story.

How are these events alike? _____

_____

Connections: Worldly Wise

Book title _____

Make two text-to-world connections.

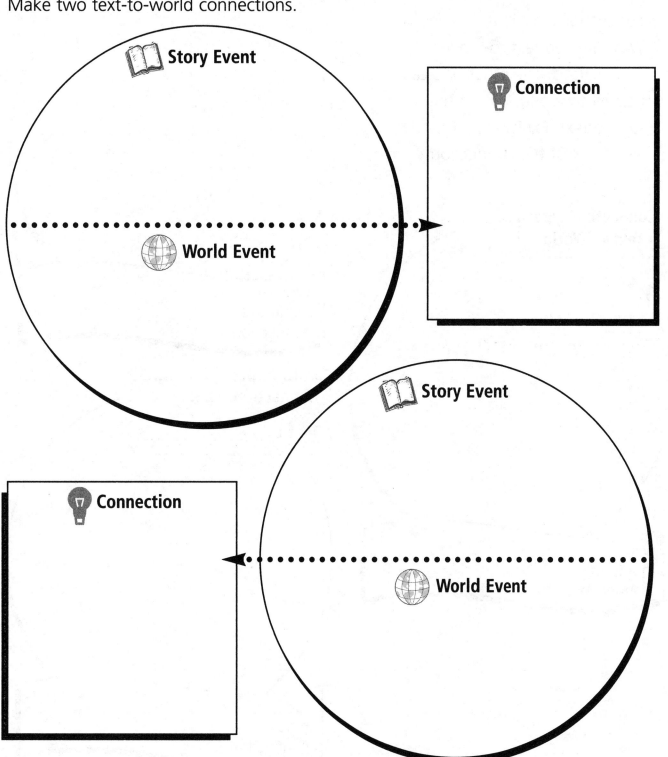

Connections: On Top of the World

As you read, write three connections inside the circles. Two must be text-to-world connections. The other one can be text to world, text to self, or text to text. Explain what made you think of the connection.

Connection type:
Text to World

Connection type:
Text to World

Why I made this connection:

Connection type:

Text to _____

Why I made this connection:

Why I made this connection:

Think-Abouts

Skill: *Monitor reading comprehension by thinking about what is read and recording those thoughts.*

Description

Readers use strategies such as predicting, explaining, elaborating, visualizing, asking questions, and drawing conclusions to interact with and understand more about their reading. However, not all readers, especially young readers, are aware that they are using strategies. "Think-abouts" help students share their thought processes and use reading strategies more actively and effectively. As they share their thoughts, students gain insight both from their metacognitive application and from the thoughts of their peers.

Getting to Know the Concept

To teach think-abouts we begin by modeling how to think aloud, and eventually guide students to write down their thoughts. When we tell children to "think about it" we really want them to analyze, dissect, synthesize information. In essence, we want them to do something by thinking. Because "thinking" is such an abstract concept, it's important to model the processes you're looking for through think-alouds. First, we need to build awareness that as we think about something, such as putting on our boots, our thoughts move on to something else that is related to the first thought. In the case of putting on boots, a child may think about the size of the boots, her last puddle-stomping experience in them, or whether they are her favorite style. From there, she might think of a pair she saw in the store and tell Mom she wants to go shopping to get new boots. This string of thoughts shows how one word may spark a connection to myriad thoughts from boots to shopping. Tell students that "thinking" is what we describe as the words and ideas in someone's head. Then unlock that thinking by making a web organizer with words and ideas related to recess (a semantic web). As the class brainstorms ideas about recess, ask each volunteer to share what made him or her think of the word he or she contributed. In this way we begin to help children understand that thoughts are sparked through connections to other thoughts.

Teaching the Concept With Literature

Continue the discussion on thinking by using a book that you have read aloud with the class. Explain to students that when we read we connect thoughts to different things and ideas, just as we do when something happens to us. Then give an example from the book. When discussing your thoughts about the book, be sure to state what in the text triggered your connection. Your explanation may go something like this:

"Yesterday, when I read *A Chair for My Mother* (Williams, 1982) I thought about a lot of different things. First, I have a jar at home that I put coins in, just like in the book. In the book they were saving for a new chair, and my husband and I are saving for a new car. When I read about the fire, I thought about how glad I am that I have never had a house fire. And finally, when Mother sat in her new chair, it made me think of my own mother when she got a new couch. She was just so excited."

Model Lesson

The goal of the lesson is to share thoughts by doing a think-aloud with the class, and to show how we can record those thoughts in a think-about. Read aloud the book *I Love Saturdays y domingos* (Ada, 2002) to the class. As you read, stop and explain your thinking, and then model the writing of these thoughts on a board or chart. This book is about a young girl who spends Saturdays with her paternal grandparents, calling them "Grandma and Grandpa," and Sundays with her mother's Hispanic parents whom she calls "Abuelita and Abuelito."

The book gives students lots to think about because they, too, have spent time with their own grandparents or relatives. Begin by just sharing your thoughts, and writing them down. Eventually, have students chime in with their thoughts. Your chart may look something like the chart below.

Continue sharing your thoughts and adding the students' thoughts as you read the book. Once again, explain that when we think, one thought connects to another and that helps us understand things, and this happens a lot when we read and begin to share our ideas with others.

For additional practice, have each student complete an organizer at his or her skill level.

What the Book Says	*My Thoughts* (with children's additions)
Both sets of grandparents are happy to see their granddaughter.	My grandparents were always happy to see me, too. My grandfather would always give me candy.
Grandma serves her milk and eggs, but Abuelita serves her papaya juice and eggs.	I don't think I would like papaya juice, but I've never had it.
Grandma has a cat, and Abuelita has a dog.	My dog is little like Abuelita's, and his name is Dustmop.
Grandma has a collection of little ceramic owls; Abuelita has real hens and chickens.	I don't think chickens are allowed in our neighborhood. Maybe Grandma can't have them either. (*My grandpa has chickens on his farm. I petted a little chick once at the petting zoo.*)
Grandma and Grandpa watch a movie about a circus; Abuelita and Abuelito take their granddaughter to a circus.	I love going to the circus. (*I went to a circus last summer and saw elephants in a parade. I saw the guy on the trapeze. I saw lots of clowns.*)

Graphic Organizers

Beginning: **I'm Thinking About . . .**
(page 28)
Students draw a scene from the book that sparked a thought as they were reading. They illustrate and write about the thought, too.

Developing: **Head in the Clouds** (page 29)
Students write about two events in the book and draw what each event made them think about.

Extending: **A Bright Idea** (page 30)
Students select three events in the book and write think-abouts.

Great Books for This Activity

Picture Books

Ada, A. (2002). *I love Saturdays y domingos.* New York: Atheneum.

Chodos-Irvine, M. (2003). *Ella Sarah gets dressed.* New York: Harcourt. A young girl makes her own fashion statement, and children connect to choosing what they wear.

Simont, M. (2001). *The stray dog.* New York: HarperCollins. A family finds a stray dog and takes him home. This sparks connections to pet ownership or a similar experience with an animal in children's lives.

Williams, V. (1982). *A Chair for my mother.* New York: Greenwillow.

Chapter Book

Kline, S. (1988). *Horrible Harry in room 2B.* New York: Viking. This book has a number of events children can relate to: Harry is in second grade, horrible things happen to him, he has a pet snake, and Halloween is coming.

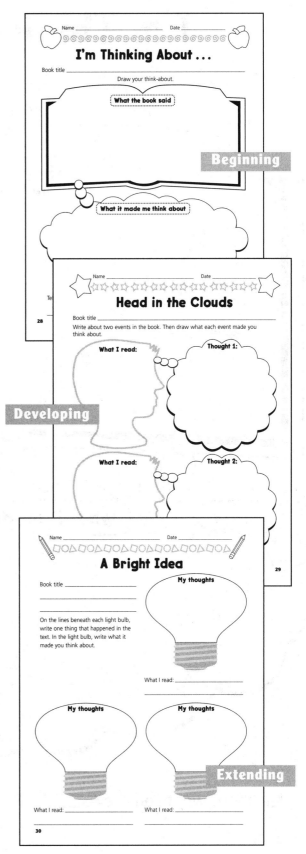

Name _____ Date _____

I'm Thinking About . . .

Book title _____

Draw your think-about.

What the book said

What it made me think about

Tell about what you drew: _____

_____

Head in the Clouds

Book title _____

Write about two events in the book. Then draw what each event made you think about.

What I read

Thought 1

What I read

Thought 2

A Bright Idea

Book title _____

_____

_____

On the lines beneath each light bulb, write one thing that happened in the text. In the light bulb, write what it made you think about.

My thoughts

What I read: _____

_____

My thoughts

What I read: _____

_____

My thoughts

What I read: _____

_____

Visualization

Skill: *Form a mental picture based on what is heard or read.*

Description

Most accomplished readers visualize while they are reading, creating mental pictures or ongoing "movies" based on information from the text. Some readers create such vivid images that they find it difficult to separate themselves from the characters in the story. Yet, we know students who, for a variety of reasons—such as focusing exclusively on decoding—don't visualize while they read, and miss out on truly understanding and enjoying what they read. Accomplished readers often monitor their comprehension by recognizing when there are flaws in the visual images they are creating. Furthermore, the ability to visualize adds aesthetic value to the act of reading; readers of all ages enjoy being able to experience vicariously the adventures of their favorite characters.

Getting to Know the Concept

You might begin visualization instruction by asking students to describe their immediate setting: What do they see when they look around the classroom, cafeteria, or schoolyard? Help them add details and create a physical description of the space. Next, make the activity slightly more abstract. Read a description of an exotic setting (perhaps from a travel brochure) and then ask some follow-up questions: "What did you 'see' as I read this description?" "What might you be riding to get around this location?" (Perhaps it would be a camel or a sailboat or a ski mobile, depending on the setting they were visualizing.) "Did you picture any people while I was reading this description? If so, what clothing were they wearing?" After some discussion, show pictures from the travel brochure. You might also select a story published in both text and DVD format, such as "Cinderella." After reading the story, you could have students orally share their visualizations and then watch the video to see how closely their interpretation of the text matched that of the DVD version.

Teaching the Concept With Literature

For this lesson, we use a book that has vivid language and excellent supporting illustrations, *Probuditi!* (Van Allsburg, 2006). This is the story of Calvin and his friend, Rodney, who hypnotize Calvin's little sister, Trudy, and change her into a dog. Having her act like a puppy is amusing at first, but the boys begin to panic when they can't get her out of her hypnotic state. Before reading the story, remind students that they should try to visualize what's happening—that is, create a picture in their minds that matches the written text. Without revealing the illustrations, read a few pages of the text and have students describe the visual images they are creating or perhaps have them use drama to depict what they are visualizing. Since Trudy, as a puppy, engages in some actions that aren't appropriate for children, such as licking Calvin's face, you might want to have students get into the position they visualize and then freeze the action.

Model Lesson

Use a book similar to Van Allsburg's, such as *The Great White Man-Eating Shark: A Cautionary Tale* (Mahy, 1989), the story of Norvin, a boy who looks and swims like a shark. One summer, he decides to use his looks to scare beachgoers away from a local cove so he can swim without having anyone get in his way. But his plan backfires.

Conceal Jonathan Allen's illustration on the cover and first page of this book. Remind students that they should create a picture in their head that matches the description the author provides and then read the first page. Stop and ask students to draw Norvin. Have students share their drawings and then reveal Allen's illustration. Continue to read until Norvin begins to make his dorsal fin. Stop and have students draw. Show Allen's illustrations. Stop once or twice more before finishing the text. When you've finished the story, explain that when visualizing, readers sometimes picture themselves in one of two

places (Parsons, 2006):

❋ Outside the story. They can see everything that is happening to everyone.

❋ Right in the book, following along with one of the characters, like a shadow. They can just see what this character sees.

Take each "view" and discuss it. If you were outside the story watching what was happening to the characters, where would you be standing? What would you see? What would you be feeling? What would be the most exciting part? Why? If you were following along with one of the characters, which character would you be with? Why would you pick this character? What would you see as you shadowed this character? What would you be thinking?

After sharing several examples of each "view," discuss what you might be able to see from one view that you couldn't see from another.

For additional practice, have each student complete an organizer at his or her skill level.

Graphic Organizers

Students may not be aware that they visualize while reading (or they may not visualize), so you may need to teach several whole-class lessons similar to the one we just modeled before students are ready for one of the following graphic organizers.

Beginning: **Picture This** (page 34)
Students stop once at a teacher-directed spot, draw what they visualize, and write about their picture.

Developing: Pausing to Make a Picture
(page 35)

Students stop once at a teacher-directed spot and identify whether they are visualizing the story from "outside the story," looking at everything, or visualizing from "inside the book," shadowing a character and seeing just what that character sees. Students draw what they visualize and write about their picture.

Extending: Pictures in My Mind
(page 36)

Students stop once at a teacher-directed spot and draw two pictures: First, they draw what they visualized from "outside the story"—seeing everything—and then from "inside the book"—seeing just what one character saw. They explain how the two pictures differed.

Great Books for This Activity

Picture Books

Mahy, M. (1989). *The great white man-eating shark: A cautionary tale.* New York: Dial.

Tompert, A. (1993). *Just a little bit.* Boston, MA: Houghton Mifflin.

Van Allsburg, C. (2006). *Probuditi!* New York: Houghton Mifflin.

Woodson, J. (1997). *We had a picnic this Sunday past.* New York: Hyperion.

Chapter Book

Danziger, P. (1994). *Amber Brown is not a crayon.* New York: G.P. Putnam's Sons.

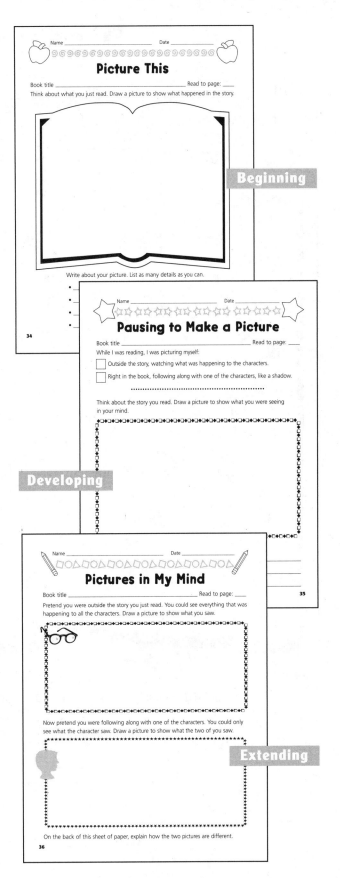

Picture This

Book title _____ Read to page: ____

Think about what you just read. Draw a picture to show what happened in the story.

Write about your picture. List as many details as you can.

- _____
- _____
- _____
- _____

Pausing to Make a Picture

Book title _____ Read to page: ____

While I was reading, I was picturing myself:

☐ Outside the story, watching what was happening to the characters.

☐ Right in the book, following along with one of the characters, like a shadow.

• •

Think about the story you read. Draw a picture to show what you were seeing in your mind.

Write about your picture.

_____

_____

_____

Pictures in My Mind

Book title _____ Read to page: ____

Pretend you were outside the story you just read. You could see everything that was happening to all the characters. Draw a picture to show what you saw.

Now pretend you were following along with one of the characters. You could only see what the character saw. Draw a picture to show what the two of you saw.

On the back of this sheet of paper, explain how the two pictures are different.

Prediction

Skill: *Use prior knowledge and information from the story to infer what might happen.*

Description

Young children predict all the time. We suspect that many children would probably be able to predict, with a fairly high degree of accuracy, which TV show their brother or sister would watch on a given day. Probably not many children, however, would be able to explain what it means to predict or what they did to arrive at their predictions. When we predict, we use our background knowledge and experience to infer what's likely to occur in the future. We figure out what's probably going to happen, given what we already know to be true. In the TV example above, the child would consider the TV choices and what he already knew about his sibling. When we read, we engage in a very similar process: we combine information from the text with our knowledge and our experiences to forecast a logical future event.

Getting to Know the Concept

We can teach the concept of prediction by preparing some "what-if" scenarios.

❉ What if it were raining out and you went for a walk in your stocking feet?

❉ What if you left a full glass of milk on the table and your cat jumped up on the table?

❉ What if a mailman delivered your mail to the wrong house?

Ask for several ideas and how students arrived at each answer.

In all these cases, we want children to begin to see that they are taking what they know and using it to make an educated guess about what might happen in the future. We say "educated guess" because one's background knowledge and experiences must be used to produce a valid guess. In some cases, more than one answer is possible. Answers are acceptable as long as they are based logically on what one already knows.

Teaching the Concept With Literature

Once your students have had some experience making predictions, it's time to introduce this concept with literature. We begin by reading aloud books that have predictable story lines, such as *Monsieur Saguette and His Baguette* (Asch, 2004). Monsieur Saguette uses his baguette in predictable ways. Using a think-aloud, tell students what knowledge or experiences you are using to infer what might happen.

Then make a prediction. Continue reading to check the accuracy of your prediction. Read some more, stop, and then have students share what they already know that would help them infer what might happen next. Have them make a prediction and then listen as you read to check their accuracy.

Model Lesson

Choose a book with familiar settings and events, such as *Gooney Bird Greene* (Lowry, 2002), a humorous chapter book about Gooney Bird Greene, a second grader who transfers into the Watertower Elementary School in October. For this lesson, you'll need a T-chart with the headings "What I Know That Can Help Me Make a Prediction" on one side and "My Prediction" on the other.

Begin the lesson by reviewing what we mean by prediction: when we make a prediction, we take information from the story and combine it with our own knowledge and experiences to figure out what might happen next. Read aloud a few pages of the book. Stop at a place where you can make a prediction. Talk through what you already know that could help you determine what might happen next. Record this

information on the left column of the T-chart. Make a prediction and record it on the right side of the T-chart. Continue reading to determine whether your prediction was accurate. Your chart might look like the one below.

Model this process several times using the T-chart. Then guide students through this same process. When appropriate, have students offer as many viable possibilities as they can generate. Emphasize that the information they use can come from a book, their experiences, or their own knowledge. For most children, prediction is easy, but providing evidence to support their predictions can be challenging.

For additional practice, have each student complete an organizer at his or her skill level.

Graphic Organizers

Beginning: **What's Next?** (page 40)
Students draw two pictures: one showing their prediction and one showing what they know that helped them make the prediction. Students read to confirm or disconfirm their prediction.

What I know that can help me make a prediction:	My prediction:

Developing: **Predicting the Future** (page 41)
Students draw a picture of their prediction and explain it. Then they write what they know that helped them make the prediction. Students read to confirm or disconfirm their prediction.

Extending: **Pictures in My Mind** (page 42)
Students draw a picture of their prediction. Then they describe what they know that helped them make the prediction. Students consider alternate predictions and write one if it seems logical. Finally, they read to confirm or disconfirm their prediction(s).

Great Books for This Activity

Picture Books

Asch, F. (2004). *Monsieur Saguette and his baguette*. Toronto: Kids Can Press.

Rylant, C. (1994). *Henry and Mudge and the careful cousin*. New York: Macmillan. There is always something happening with Henry and Mudge. It takes careful reading to find out what.

Tyler, L. W. (1987). *Waiting for mom*. New York: Viking. Will mother ever come? Predict throughout the book and then read on to find out.

Titherington, J. (1986). *Pumpkin, pumpkin*. New York: Greenwillow. This book follows the path of a young girl in a pumpkin patch.

Chapter Book

Lowry, L. (2002). *Gooney Bird Green*. New York: Houghton Mifflin.

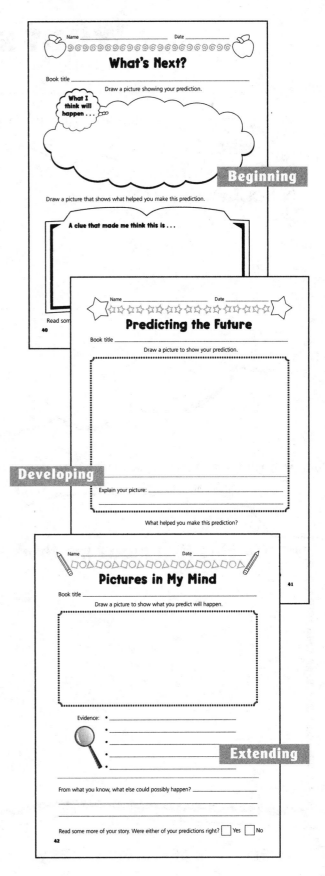

Name _____ Date _____

What's Next?

Book title _____

Draw a picture showing your prediction.

What I think will happen . . .

Draw a picture that shows what helped you make this prediction.

A clue that made me think this is . . .

Read some more of your story. Was your prediction right? ☐ Yes ☐ No

Name _____ Date _____

Predicting the Future

Book title _____

Draw a picture to show your prediction.

Explain your picture: _____

_____

What helped you make this prediction?

• _____

• _____

• _____

Read some more of your story. Was your prediction right? ☐ Yes ☐ No

Pictures in My Mind

Book title _____

Draw a picture to show what you predict will happen.

Evidence:
- _____
- _____
- _____
- _____
- _____

From what you know, what else could possibly happen? _____

_____

_____

Read some more of your story. Were either of your predictions right? ☐ Yes ☐ No

Character

Skill: *Describe a character by physical characteristics and personality.*

Description

At the primary level, character can be defined as the "outside" and "inside" of a person in the story. The "outside" is described by the character's appearance and any distinguishable mannerisms or physical characteristics belonging to that character, such as a grandfather with a bent back. The "inside" of the character, his or her personality, is reflected by the way the character behaves and thinks and feels about other people or incidents. Picture books are a great avenue to study both the physical description (outside characteristics) and the personality (inside characteristics) of a character. Pictures often clearly depict what a character looks like, and readers can often imply from a character's expression or gestures what the character is feeling. Understanding characters is the foundation for making inferences about motives.

Getting to Know the Concept

Hands-on experiences with the "outside" (physical description) of a character make this concept easier to teach to primary-grade children. Begin by modeling with a description of a teddy bear or similar stuffed animal. Write on the board what you see, and students will automatically begin to chime in. For instance, a panda's physical description may look like this:

White and black fur	4 legs	2 charcoal eyes	Small nose
Wide mouth	Round belly	Large animal	Wears bow around neck!

Solicit class input as you model, using different stuffed animals. You might extend the lesson by having students do the same task with a partner, using stuffed animals they bring from home.

Once children are comfortable giving a physical description of their stuffed animals, use photographs or pictures of people wearing a variety of expressions to begin to build the concept of "inside" characteristics or personality traits. Share action pictures or expressive faces with students and ask them to explain how they think the pictured character feels. Now have them apply their inferring skills to cartoon or movie characters, such as Mickey Mouse and Cinderella. Use leading questions and oral cloze procedures to help children infer characteristics from actions and dialogue (e.g., How did Cinderella act toward her stepsisters and the animals?). List their ideas on the T-chart. Your chart might look like the one on page 44.

Depending on how well students are grasping the concept of character personality traits, you may want to repeat this activity a few times with other familiar characters from movies they have seen.

Teaching the Concept With Literature

Once students understand how to describe the inside and outside of characters, it is time to help them apply this concept to literary characters. Start with familiar characters from series books such as Clifford, Franklin, or Encyclopedia Brown to simplify this exercise. In short books the character is not usually well developed, but series books allow characters to become more familiar to children.

Model Lesson

Horace and Morris but Mostly Dolores (Howe, 1999) is a good book to use to help students easily grasp the feelings of the main character, Dolores. In this book Dolores and two her friends love adventure, but the friends split up when the boys join the "boy" club and Dolores joins the "girl" club. Eventually, the friends reunite to go exploring.

We use a four-piece graphic organizer to help students gather a range of details. Share with students the four parts of the chart shown on page 45 (outside: body and clothes, facial expressions; inside: feelings and action), and tell them that as you read the book you want them to listen for sentences that describe Dolores, how she feels, and what she does. Before reading, have students look at Dolores on the first page and describe her looks and expression. Write down students' observations on the graphic organizer. After reading the story, have students tell you what they remember. If necessary, reread the story to aid students in adding to the graphic organizer. When the students tell you what Dolores does and what her facial expressions are, ask what these reveal about Dolores. Your finished product will look something like the chart on page 45.

Remind students that we can figure out what characters are like when we read about how they feel about things and take notice of what they do.

For additional practice, have each student complete an organizer at his or her skill level.

Graphic Organizers

Beginning: **Outside In** (page 46)
Students draw and write what a character looks like, and what a character does.

Developing: **In Character** (page 47)
Students draw and write what the character looks like and what he or she is doing, and thinking, and then they write what this tells them about the character.

Extending: **What a Character!** (page 48)
Students fill in a description of a character by focusing on both physical and emotional elements.

Character Chart

Outside	Inside
beautiful	really nice
girl	hard-working
long blonde hair	friendly
sparkling blue eyes	thoughtful
cheerful smile	smart
glass slippers	patient

Great Books for This Activity

Picture Books

Berenstain, S. & J. Berenstain bears series. These books have characters that are familiar to students.

Dr. Seuss. (1957). *The cat in the hat*. New York: Houghton Mifflin. Everyone loves this cat.

Howe, J. (1999). *Horace and Doris but mostly Delores*. New York: Atheneum.

Chapter Book

Lobel, A. (1970). Frog and toad series. New York: HarperCollins. Any of these chapter/picture books is useful as the characters are known to the students.

Dolores

Outside

Body: mouse, large white eyes, little teeth, black nose
Facial expressions: happy, excited, sad, bored

Wearing: flower in hair, striped shirt, red overall shorts, purple shoes, white shoelaces, striped socks

Inside

Feels: loves adventure, downhearted (sad), lonely, bored

Action:	Shows s/he is . . .
sails and climbs	brave
went to girls' club	resourceful
makes new friend	friendly

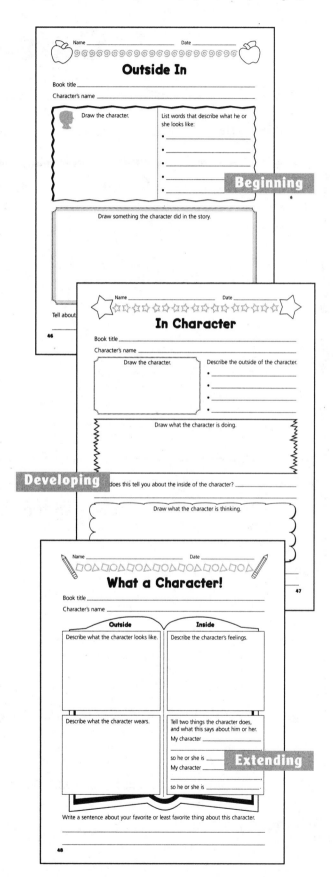

Name _____ Date _____

Outside In

Book title _____

Character's name _____

Draw the character.

List words that describe what he or she looks like:

- _____
- _____
- _____
- _____
- _____

Draw something the character did in the story.

Tell about your picture: _____

_____

In Character

Book title _____

Character's name _____

Draw the character.	Describe the outside of the character.

- _____

- _____

- _____

- _____

Draw what the character is doing.

What does this tell you about the inside of the character? _____

_____

Draw what the character is thinking.

What does this tell you about the inside of the character? _____

_____

What a Character!

Book title _____

Character's name _____

Outside	**Inside**
Describe what the character looks like.	Describe the character's feelings.
Describe what the character wears.	Tell two things the character does, and what this says about him or her. My character _____ _____, so he or she is _____ . My character _____ _____, so he or she is _____ .

Write a sentence about your favorite or least favorite thing about this character.

_____

_____

Setting

Skill: *Describe setting as a place where the events of a story happen.*

Description

For young children, setting can be defined as "where the story takes place," or as "where things happen in the story." As we strive to help emergent or developing readers understand place, it helps to include the fives senses—what the children might see, hear, smell, taste, or feel if they could jump into the pages of the book and interact with the objects mentioned in the story. Keeping the senses in mind aids students in seeing the whole picture or scene within the story.

Getting to Know the Concept

A sensory experience allows students to comprehend setting as a place. Gather students together in a group and take them to three or four different places in the school, or as you take the students to gym or music, take a detour and discuss the place or setting in which you stop. For example, take your students to the hallway outside of the music room and ask questions about the "setting" you are in. What do the walls of the hall look like? The floor? Ceiling? How do the walls feel to their touch? What can be heard? Children walking? Singing from the music room? Is there a smell that seems particular to the music room? Repeat this procedure at different places inside or outside the school, such as the cafeteria, the library, the playground, and the gym.

After the sensory experience, bring the children back to the room. Tell them you are going to describe a place that could be a setting in a story and they are going to try to guess what that setting is. Then proceed to give hints describing the places you have just visited. For example: "I am in a huge room, and I see children sitting at tables and they are eating lunch. There is a mix of smells like peanut butter, tuna fish, and chocolate milk." Have the children guess where you are. Explain that when children read about a cafeteria in a story, the author gives similar hints, and that the place in a story is called the setting. Do this with other areas you visited and continue to emphasize the word *setting*.

Tell students that books can be like the riddles you have been enjoying. Sometimes in a story the author tells you where the setting is, and other times you have to solve a riddle to figure out the setting. You need to look at the pictures and listen to what the author is saying because sometimes the pictures show what is happening, but not where it's happening, and that's when you need to solve the riddle.

It is helpful for the reader to think about what can be seen, heard, smelled, touched, or tasted to help figure out the setting.

If students need more practice comprehending setting, use pictures as a tool to explain book settings. Simple pictures from magazines can be shown to students and the setting and the details in the pictures discussed.

Teaching the Concept With Literature

Once students have the concept of setting, it is time to explore it further with books. In some books the setting is easy to identify either by the pictures or words. One simple book to begin with is *Click, Clack, Moo: Cows That Type* (Cronin, 2000). In this book all of the action takes place on a farm and the setting is very important. We will use this book in the following lesson.

Model Lesson

Prior to reading the book, remind students that a setting is where the story takes place. Tell them that as you read they should think about where the story happens and how that might be important. Tell them to visualize the place and to think about what they might see, hear, smell, taste, or feel.

Read aloud the book, stopping at various times to elaborate upon the setting through discussion. You might say, "There is a farmer in the story, so where might this story take place?" As you read on, you might comment, "The cows are in a barn. Boys and girls, where would we find a barn?" And by answering the "riddles" students will discover the setting.

After reading the story with the class, together fill in a sense graphic organizer on the board or chart paper. It might look like the chart below.

Discuss with the class how to fill in the different parts of the graphic organizer, and explain that when describing the setting an author may not evoke all the senses. Fill in as many boxes as you can. When you've completed the organizer, have students share sentences using a word from the graphic organizer to describe the setting.

For additional practice, have each student complete an organizer at his or her skill level.

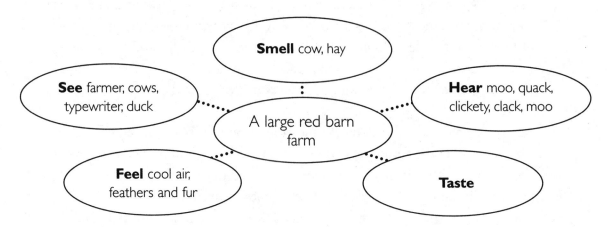

Graphic Organizers

Beginning: **Place Mats** (page 52)
Students draw a picture of the setting and generate words to describe what they "see" in the story's setting.

Developing: **A Sense of Place** (page 53)
Students draw sensory details from the book. Then they use some of these details to draw the setting and write a sentence about it.

Extending: **Sensing the Setting** (page 54)
Students list as many sensory details from the setting as they can. Then they draw a picture, and using their senses, write a description of the setting.

Great Books for This Activity

Picture Books

Cronin, D. (2000). *Click, clack, moo: Cows that type*. New York: Simon & Schuster.

Layton, N. (1998). *Smile if you're human.* New York: Scholastic. This story has only one setting, but children must guess what the story line is to determine the setting.

Willems, M. (2005). *Knuffle bunny*. New York: Hyperion. A city is the main setting, but the action takes place at various spots, and camera pictures are used with character drawings superimposed.

Chapter Book

Roop, C. & Roop, P. (1985). *Keep the lights burning, Abbie*. Minneapolis, MN: Carolrhoda Books. The lighthouse setting is wonderfully described and extremely important in this story's plot.

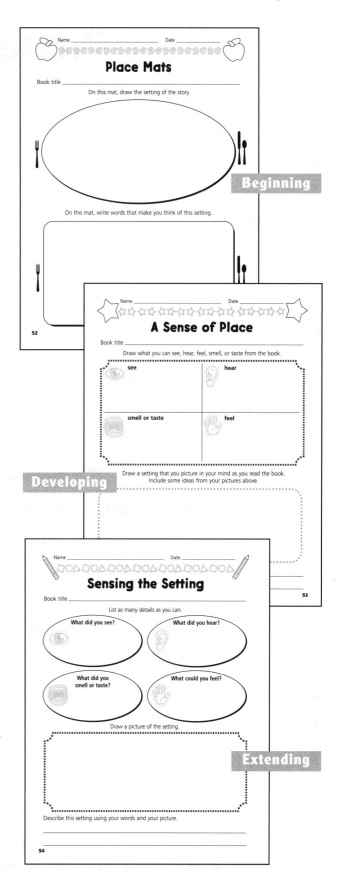

Place Mats

Book title _____

On this mat, draw the setting of the story.

On this mat, write words that make you think of this setting.

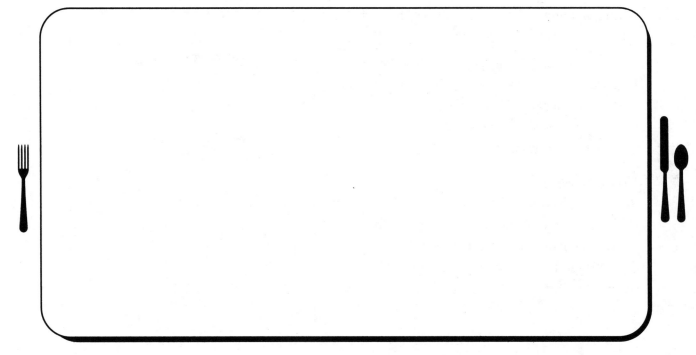

A Sense of Place

Book title _____

Draw what you can see, hear, feel, smell, or taste from the book.

see	 hear
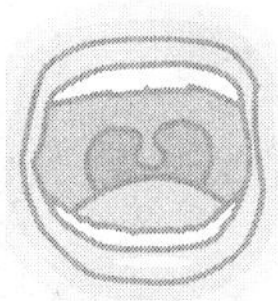 **smell or taste**	 **feel**

Draw a setting that you picture in your mind as you read the book.
Include some ideas from your pictures above.

Describe this setting: _____

_____

Name _____   Date _____

Sensing the Setting

Book title _____

List as many details as you can.

What did you see?

What did you hear?

What did you smell or taste?

What could you feel?

Draw a picture of the setting.

Describe this setting using your words and your picture.

_____

_____

Plot

Skill: *Identify that the problem and solution make up the plot.*

Description

The plot of a story includes the problem, attempts to solve the problem, and the solution. For some story lines the plot may best be described as comprising the characters' goals, attempts to achieve these goals, and the outcome. Not all books have a plot, however. Some have a "straight story line," meaning there is no rising action or a climax within the story. For instance, the book *In the Small, Small Pond* (Fleming, 1993) colorfully describes actions and natural elements within and near the pond, but there is no rising action. In contrast, the old favorite, *The Little Engine That Could* (Piper, 1930), lets us know that if we believe in ourselves anything is possible. The young engine's goals of reaching his destination, and the achieved outcome, dictate the plot. When teaching plot, it is important to select books that have simple plots which young children can easily identify.

Getting to Know the Concept

To understand plot, children must learn and be able to identify the three different concepts that form the plot, and be able to name these as the problem, attempts to solve the problem, and the solution. Using classroom scenarios to help students identify each of these components works well. Begin by building the concept of problem and solution with familiar classroom issues. For instance, ask students how to solve the following problems (and have them add a few of their own problems to the list):

❀ You have a full trash can but still have more trash to throw away.

❀ You have forgotten your lunch money.

❀ You need a pencil, but you can only find an unsharpened pencil.

Focus on the problems that have more than one solution and, using one of the examples given, explain that sometimes it takes more than one try to solve a problem.

Then stage a "real" problem. Tell students that you cannot find your cell phone and that this is a problem because you will need it after school. Create a chart like this one.

Problem: Can't find cell phone
Attempts to solve: (1) Teacher looks around desk
(2) Students look around their desks
(3) Teacher calls her cell phone
Solution: Children hear ring, cell phone is found

Use it to aid in building this concept with students. First, fill in the problem. Then look around your desk, and tell the students you couldn't find it there. Write this down as an attempt to solve your problem. Then have them look around their desk areas. Write this down as the second attempt. Finally use your room phone or a colleague's cell phone to call your cell phone and ask students to listen for the ring. Allow them to "find" the phone, and fill in the solution.

Teaching the Concept With Literature

Plot is complicated, and students will most likely need repeated instruction on this concept in order to gain a solid understanding. When using literature examples to teach plot, it might be best to begin with a simple story that children can easily follow, such as *Are You My Mother?* (Eastman, 1960) or "The Last Story" from the George and Martha series (Marshall, 1972). Both of these stories are very short and have one problem, and a simple solution. Proceed to more difficult plots, with more attempts to solve the problem, but always use books that focus more on plot than on character development. Continue building the concept of plot as the problem, attempts to solve the problem, and the solution by reading simple stories that clearly follow this format and discussing the story components.

Model Lesson

Once students have shown success identifying simple plots, it is time to give a directed lesson using a slightly more complicated story like *Hilda Must Be Dancing* (Wilson, 2004). This delightful story focuses on the problem of Hilda Hippo's dancing which disturbs the jungle neighborhood. After a series of attempts to stop her from dancing, Hilda discovers a solution.

Remind students that the plot of a story tells us the problem, how the characters are trying to solve the problem, and the solution. After reading *Hilda Must Be Dancing* to the class, review the story by having students help you fill in a chart like the one below. Once the chart has been completed, ask students how the setting helped with the solution. In this case Hilda discovered she could use a lake or pond to dance without disturbing others. Explain that sometimes the setting is very important to the plot of the story. Extend the discussion by asking students what other ways the jungle animals might have gotten Hilda to stop dancing.

For additional practice, have each student complete an organizer at his or her skill level.

Hilda Must Be Dancing Plot Chart

Problem: Hilda Hippo's friends don't like all the shaking and the bumps and thumps when she dances.
Attempts to solve: The monkeys talk her into taking up knitting. The rhinos try to get her to sing. The water buffalo try to get her to take up swimming.
Solution: When Hilda begins swimming she finds she can do water ballet. This makes everyone happy.

Graphic Organizers

Beginning: **Spot the Plot** (page 58)
Students draw and write about the problem, an attempt to solve it, and the solution.

Developing: **Plotting the Plot** (page 59)
Students write about the problem, two or three attempts to solve it, and the solution. They identify who caused the problem and who solved it.

Extending: **Story-Lining the Plot** (page 60)
Students write about the problem, three attempts to solve it, and the solution. Then they offer a solution of their own. Lastly, they explain which solution is better, theirs or the author's.

Great Books for This Activity

Picture Books

DePaola, T. (1975). *Strega Nona*. New York: Simon & Schuster.
This well-known tale describes Anthony's problem after stealing Strega Nona's magic pot.

Eastman, P. (1960). *Are you my mother?* New York: Random House.

Marshall, J. (1972). *George and Martha*. New York: Houghton Mifflin.

Piper, W. (1930). *The little engine that could*. New York: Platt & Munk.

Wilson, K. (2004). *Hilda must be dancing*. New York: Simon and Schuster.

Chapter Book

Higginson, H. (2006). *Keeker and the sneaky pony*. San Francisco: Chronicle Books.
The main problem in this book occurs when Keeker's new pony, Plum, runs away from her in the woods.

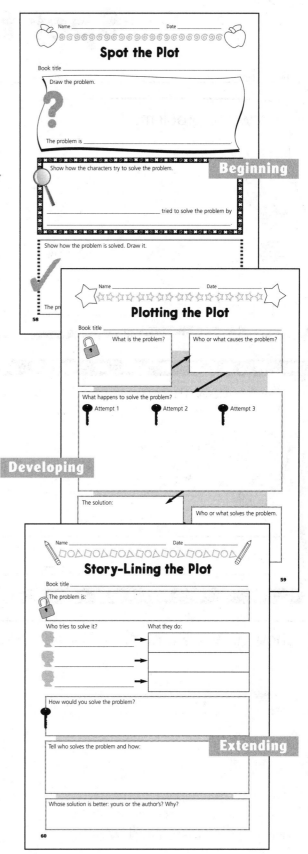

Spot the Plot

Book title _____

Draw the problem.

The problem is _____.

Show how the characters try to solve the problem.

_____ tried to solve the problem by

_____.

Show how the problem is solved. Draw it.

The problem is solved when _____.

Name _____ Date _____

Plotting the Plot

Book title _____

🔓 What is the problem?	Who or what causes the problem?

What happens to solve the problem?

🔑 Attempt 1   🔑 Attempt 2   🔑 Attempt 3

The solution:

Who or what solves the problem:

Story-Lining the Plot

Book title _____

The problem is:

Who tries to solve it?   What they do:

_____ →

_____ →

_____ →

How would you solve the problem?

Tell who solves the problem and how.

Whose solution is better: yours or the author's? Why?

Story Maps

Skill: *Recall the character, setting, problem and solution of a story.*
(Teach this lesson after you have introduced characters, setting, and plot.)

Description

Story maps allow readers to see the components of a story and answer who, what, where, when, and why questions. A basic story map usually contains spaces for the main characters, the setting, the problem, the attempts to solve the problem, and the solution. For the primary level these elements are simplified to character, setting, problem, and solution. The story map aids students in recalling an outline of the story by identifying the character(s), setting, and plot and organizing this information on one graphic organizer. When children can recall and discuss these four areas, they are at the beginning stages of learning how to create a written retelling of a story, and therefore story mapping is an effective strategy to help children improve their retelling skills.

Getting to Know the Concept

Once the lessons on characters, setting, and plot have been taught, children begin to understand that all of these components together form a story. A review of each component may be necessary, and can be done using actual experiences from students in the class—Kiera's forgetting her lunch, for example, or Joshua's misplacing his homework. Make a story map to fill in the "story" or "stories" as children share their experiences. A map on Kiera and Joshua may look something like this:

Character	Kiera	Joshua
Setting	school	home
Problem	Kiera forgot her lunch money and would not be able to eat lunch.	Joshua couldn't find his homework.
Solution	The cafeteria workers gave Kiera a peanut butter and jelly sandwich.	Joshua and his mother looked all over the house and found it under a bag full of groceries.

As you listen and write down the components of the children's stories, have students tell you under which category each piece of information should fall. After a story has been plotted on the story map, have students share other ways the problem could have been solved.

Teaching the Concept With Literature

Begin teaching story mapping skills with very simple stories. Some stories, although filled with wonderful, vibrant vocabulary, such as *In the Tall, Tall Grass* (Fleming, 1991), are not appropriate for story maps because their straight story line shows no rising action. Stories selected for teaching this skill need to have a story line in which the characters, setting, problem, and solution are simple and readily identifiable, such as *Are You My Mother?* (Eastman, 1960).

Model Lesson

Begin with a read-aloud using a book with a simple story line such as *Little Critter's The Picnic* (Mayer, 1988). In this delightful tale the Critters attempt to have an old-fashioned picnic but have trouble finding the perfect spot.

Prepare a story map listing character, setting, problem, and solution. Read the story aloud, and after reading as a class, fill in the components, being sure to discuss and include details. Your story map will resemble the one below.

For additional practice, have each student complete an organizer at his or her skill level.

Graphic Organizers

Beginning: **Super Story Map** (page 64)
Students draw and label the main character, setting, problem, and solution.

Developing: **No Napping, Story Mapping** (page 65)
Students draw and give details about the main character, the setting, the problem, and the solution.

Extending: **Story Map Scenario** (page 66)
Students identify the main characters, discuss and draw the setting, and write the problem and the solution. In addition, students generate solutions of their own.

Great Books for This Activity

Picture Books
Cazzola, G. (1991). *The bells of Santa Lucia.* New York: Philomel. A young girl loses her grandmother and stays inside because she does not want to hear bells.

Character	Setting	Problem	Solution
The Critters	Outside, then in the house during the day	The critters want to have a picnic but can't find a good spot.	After going from the stream to the field to the cave, they decide to have their picnic inside their house.

Eastman, P. (1960). *Are you my mother?* New York: Random House.

Mayer, M. (1988). *Little Critter's the picnic.* New York: Golden Books.

Preller, J. (1994). *Wake me in spring.* New York: Scholastic. Poor bear wants to sleep for the winter, and mouse wants him to stay awake.

Chapter Book

Kline, S. (1998). *Horrible Harry moves up to third grade.* New York:Viking. Things have changed for Harry in third grade, and he's not sure if he likes it.

Also Cited

Fleming, D. (1991). *In the tall, tall grass.* New York: Henry Holt.

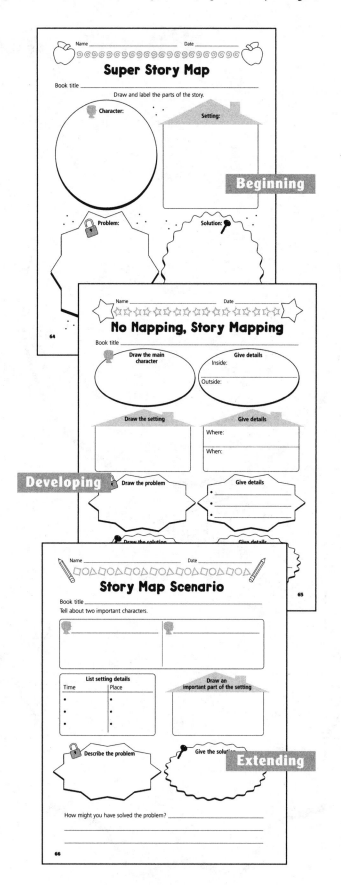

Name _____ Date _____

Super Story Map

Book title _____

Draw and label the parts of the story.

Character

Setting

Problem

Solution

No Napping, Story Mapping

Book title _____

Draw the main character

Give details

Inside:

Outside:

Draw the setting

Give details

Where:

When:

Draw the problem

Give details

- _____
- _____
- _____

Draw the solution

Give details

- _____
- _____
- _____

Story Map Scenario

Book title _____

Tell about two important characters.

List setting details

Time	Place
•	•
•	•
•	•

Draw an important part of the setting

Describe the problem

Give the solution

How might you have solved the problem? _____

_____

_____

Details

Skill: Examine how authors use details to provide specific information.

Description

For more advanced readers, details can refer to extended sentences that support a main idea, but at this level, we want students to simply understand that a detail is a piece of information or a fact used to describe a person, place, thing, or event. Authors use details to reveal information. We use the term *details* with students because they will hear this word used in different contexts throughout the school day: They are asked to list details when observing nature in a science lesson, for instance, or use details in their writing to expand an idea, or provide details about a playground incident to help resolve a dispute.

Getting to Know the Concept

We teach the concept of *details* by using interesting objects around a classroom—a class pet or a flowering plant. We take one object and have students tell what they know about the object. They might say, for instance, that Chester, their guinea pig, likes to burrow into shredded paper. We record this detail on a chart and invite students to add other details about Chester. They might say that he has no tail; he is soft; he makes loud noises. When you introduce this skill, see if students can provide details that relate to all the senses. Explain that these details provide us with important information about the object.

Try this same exercise with a place. Take a walk outside, if possible, or to the nurse's office, or even take in the view from your classroom window. Have students suggest details that would help someone else understand what they are seeing, hearing, feeling, smelling, and if appropriate, tasting. Have them try to make the details as specific and informative as possible.

Finally, try this exercise with events. Have a student hop across the room while the other students observe. What did they notice? You might prompt with questions such as: Did the student hop on one foot or two? Did the student pause to catch his balance? Did he smile or look serious? Did you feel anything when he hopped past you? Did the floor shake or did his shoulder touch yours? What did you hear? Laughter? Clapping? Explain that when they are using these descriptive words, students are providing details that help someone who wasn't there enjoy the event too!

Teaching the Concept With Literature

Once your students understand that details are important or interesting pieces of information, it's time to introduce this concept with literature. Depending on the developmental level of the students in your class, you might decide to spend some time introducing details with a picture book, such as Banks's *The Nightwalker* (2000), stopping as you read so you and your students can talk about the details you notice in either the pictures or the text. Talk with the students about how the details supply information about the story you are reading.

Model Lesson

Flat Stanley (Brown, 1964) is a book that has stood the test of time; children have laughed at Stanley's antics for more than forty years. For this lesson, you'll need a piece of chart paper divided into four sections. Put one of the following words in each section: *People, Places, Things, Events.*

If your students are not familiar with *Flat Stanley*, read it aloud simply to enjoy the story line. On a subsequent reading, stop periodically to recall some of the details the author has included. For example, you might note that a bulletin board fell on Stanley as he slept, which caused him to become flat. Record this detail in the Events category. You might point out that Stanley is four feet tall, about a foot wide, and half an inch thick. Record this in the People category. Provide examples of details that fit into each of the four categories, when possible. Your chart might look something like the one below.

Conclude the lesson by explaining to students that if you change one detail in a book, the entire story could change. Suggest, for example, that if you changed Stanley from a boy who is half an inch thick to a boy who is six inches thick, he would weigh more and probably would not be able to go some of the places he went. Have them consider the impact of this and other possible changes. Explain that details are important because they shape how we think about characters, settings, objects, and events in the stories we read.

For additional practice, have each student complete an organizer at his or her skill level.

People	*Stanley*: 4 ft. tall, 1 ft. wide, 1/2 in. thick
Places	Stanley's room, school, sewer, art museum
Things	bulletin board, ring, painting, bike pump
Events	Bulletin board fell on him and flattened him

Graphic Organizers

Beginning: **Drawing Details** (page 70)
Students draw a detailed picture about a person, place, thing, or event from the story they are reading. Then they label the details in their picture.

Developing: **Detail Detective** (page 71)
Students find details in the story they are reading and record them in the appropriate magnifying glasses.

Extending: **Detail Delivery** (page 72)
Students place details from the story they are reading into the following categories: people, places, things, or events. Then, they select one detail from each category that they would like to change and indicate the impact this change would have on the story line.

Great Books for This Activity

Picture Books

Banks, K. (2000). *The night walker.* NY: Farrar Straus Giroux.

Brown, J. (1964). *Flat Stanley.* New York: Harper & Row.

dePaola, T. (2000). *Jamie O'Rourke and the pooka.* New York: G.P. Putnam's Sons.

Chapter Book

Guest, E. H. (2003). *Iris and Walter: The school play.* New York: Gulliver Books.

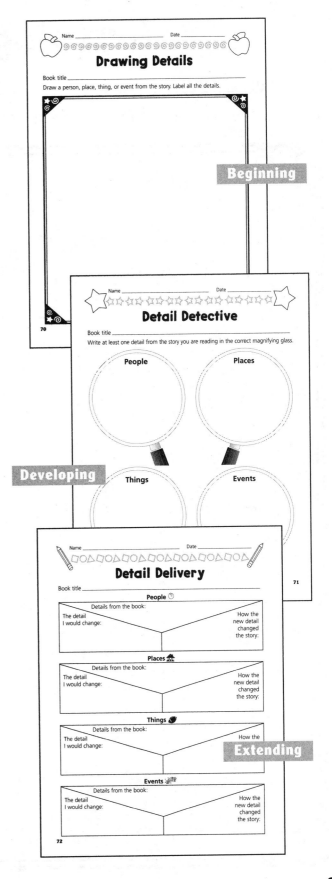

Drawing Details

Book title _____

Draw a person, place, thing, or event from the story. Label all the details.

Detail Detective

Book title _____

Write at least one detail from the story you are reading in the correct magnifying glass.

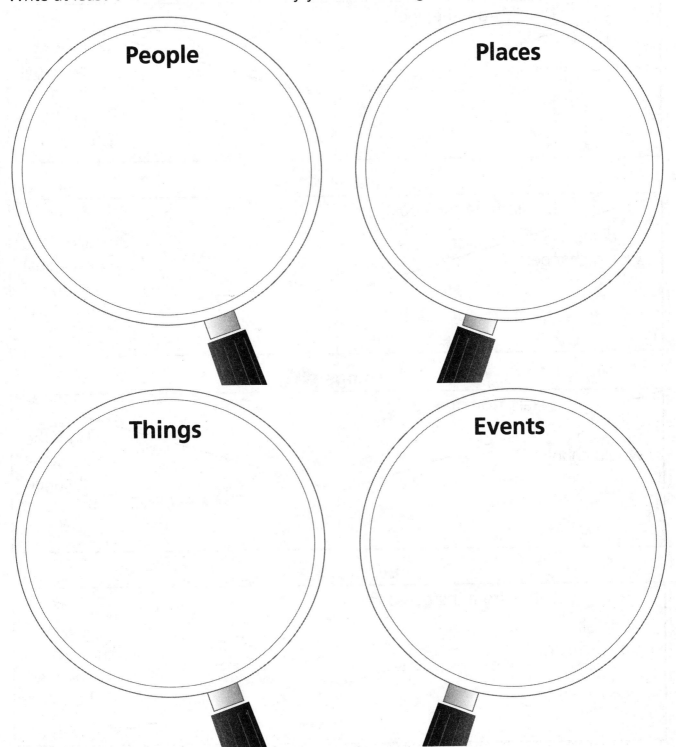

People

Places

Things

Events

Name _____   Date _____

Detail Delivery

Book title _____

People 🙂

Details from the book:

The detail
I would change:

How the
new detail
changed
the story:

Places 🏠

Details from the book:

The detail
I would change:

How the
new detail
changed
the story:

Things 🏈

Details from the book:

The detail
I would change:

How the
new detail
changed
the story:

Events 🌠

Details from the book:

The detail
I would change:

How the
new detail
changed
the story:

Compare

Skill: *Notice and describe similarities in people, places, things, or actions.*

Description

Although the term *compare* is sometimes used to specify both similarities and differences, we make a distinction between *compare* and *contrast* (described in the next lesson, pages 79–84). Compare specifies similarities; contrast specifies differences. When we teach children to compare two items, we are helping them think critically. In order to compare, students must make evaluative decisions while reading, listening, or viewing. Primary-grade students may not yet know the term *compare*, a word they will encounter often in academic settings, but they probably won't have too much trouble with this concept once you have introduced it to them using the lesson ideas below.

Getting to Know the Concept

For this lesson, you'll want to find two objects that have obvious similarities. You might use puppets, stuffed animals, small toys, classroom plants, or you might take the class on a walk to the teachers' room to compare two similar coffee mugs or outside to compare two cars in the parking lot. Talk about how the objects are alike. Encourage children to use the word "both" to signal similarities.

After introducing comparison with concrete objects, you may want to repeat this process with photographs, which are slightly more abstract. If possible, consider not only the physical characteristics (both girls have pigtails, sneakers, backpacks) but also the less obvious similarities that you can infer (both probably ride the school bus because they are walking toward a bus that's parked in front of the building).

Teaching the Concept With Literature

Once your students have had some experience making comparisons, it's time to introduce this concept with literature. Begin by reading aloud books that have wonderful characters with similar attributes, such as *The Relatives Came* by Cynthia Rylant (2001). As you read and enjoy the illustrations, discuss how the relatives from Virginia were similar to the relatives they visited.

Model Lesson

Books that offer comparisons between engaging characters or events are great choices for this lesson. One of our favorites, *Officer Buckle and Gloria* (Rathmann, 1995), is a humorous picture book about a safety officer and Gloria, a police dog, who travel around teaching children safety rules. Begin the lesson by reviewing the meaning of *compare*: when we compare, we look for ways in which the people, places, things, or events are similar. Read *Officer Buckle and Gloria*, stopping periodically to think aloud about how Officer Buckle and Gloria are alike. On chart paper, write the characters' names and list common characteristics. A partial list might look something like this:

<u>Both Officer Buckle and Gloria</u>

❋ work for the police department

❋ want children to be safe

❋ wear stars to show they work for the police department

❋ get lots of mail from children

❋ visit children in schools

❋ enjoy eating ice cream

Next, explain that readers often make comparisons between themselves and the characters in books they are reading. Doing so helps readers relate to the characters and enhances comprehension. Think aloud as you identify how you and the characters in this book are similar. Record similarities at the bottom of your list. The additional items might look like this:

❋ Officer Buckle, Gloria, and I think it's important to follow safety tips.

❋ Officer Buckle, Gloria, and I get lonely when we aren't with people we love.

❋ Officer Buckle and I wear eyeglasses.

Finally, explain that when readers get to know characters well, they can imagine other ways in which the characters might be similar to each other. For example, since we know that Officer Buckle and Gloria talk about safety rules but don't always follow them (Officer Buckle stands on a chair and Gloria does back flips), both of them probably have accidents. See if students can make additional inferences.

For additional practice, have each student complete an organizer at his or her skill level.

Graphic Organizers

Beginning: **So Much Alike** (page 76) Students identify and compare two characters and draw two pictures that show similarities.

Developing: **Just Like Me** (page 77) Students identify and compare two characters, create a list of similarities, and make one comparison between one or both characters and themselves.

Extending: **Searching for Similarities** (page 78) Students draw four or five comparisons between two characters and note whether someone they know is similar.

Great Books for This Activity

Picture Books

Ericsson, J. A. (2005). *Home to me, home to you*. New York: Little, Brown. Compare the little girl to her mother, who is on her way home from a business trip.

Rathmann, P. (1995). *Officer Buckle and Gloria*. New York: G.P. Putnam's Sons.

Stevenson, J. (1986). *No friends*. New York: William Morrow. Compare Grandpa's childhood experience of having no friends to that of Mary Ann and Louie.

Chapter Book

Rylant, C. (2001). *The relatives came*. New York: Simon and Schuster. Compare Mr. Putter to Mrs. Teaberry. This humorous book allows students to connect to relatives who are different.

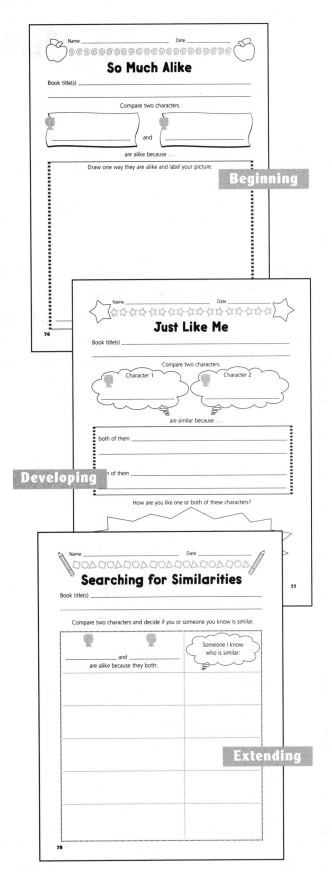

So Much Alike

Book title(s) _____

_____

Compare two characters.

and

are alike because . . .

Draw one way they are alike and label your picture.

_____

Just Like Me

Book title(s) _____

_____

Compare two characters.

Character 1

Character 2

are similar because . . .

both of them _____

_____

both of them _____

_____

How are you like one or both of these characters?

_____ and I _____

_____

_____

Searching for Similarities

Book title(s) _____

_____

Compare two characters and decide if you or someone you know is similar.

_____ and _____ are alike because they both:	Someone I know who is similar:

Contrast

Skill: *Notice and describe differences in people, places, things, or events.*
(This lesson should be taught after the previous lesson on comparing.)

Description

When we evaluate how two people, places, things, or events differ, we contrast them. Primary-grade students may not be familiar with the academic term *contrast* or the skill it represents. Since students often find it easier to look for similarities than differences, we recommend you begin by teaching comparing (similarities), then contrasting (differences), and finally comparing and contrasting together.

Your students will probably hear the term *contrast* used across the curriculum (e.g., contrast character A with character B; contrast living things with nonliving things; contrast the first day of school with the 100th day). They may also hear the word *contrast* (or *compare and contrast*) used to describe an organizational text structure in informational texts. Authors of science books, for instance, might use a contrast text structure to note differences among the sun, moon, and planets. Whenever relevant, use the word contrast in your daily language with primary-grade students so they become familiar with this term.

Getting to Know the Concept

You might teach the concept of contrast by using common objects, items you have in your classroom. For example, you might want to return to the objects you used for the lesson on compare and now focus on how they differ. If you are starting fresh, you might want to contrast two pieces of fruit—a banana and an orange, for instance—two objects with obvious differences. Remind students that you will use your five senses, when appropriate, to identify differences. Record your thinking on a T-chart. It might look something like this:

A Banana	An Orange
yellow	orange
long and thin	round
no seeds	sometimes has seeds
weak smell	strong smell

Teaching the Concept With Literature

Once your students understand what *contrast* means (that we are looking for differences in the people, places, things, or events), it's time to introduce this concept with literature. Using picture books to reinforce the concept of *contrast* allows students to use both the visual cues and the written text to identify differences. *The Witches' Supermarket* (Meddaugh, 1991) is a humorous picture book about the experiences of a little girl and her dog who inadvertently end up in a supermarket for witches on Halloween. With this book, you could contrast settings—the supermarket in the story with your local supermarket.

Model Lesson

As with the compare lesson, look for books that invite a close analysis of two elements together. We use *Bus Riders* (Denslow, 1993), which provides opportunities for students to contrast Lee, the usual school bus driver, with Thelma S., Willie, and Mr. Dodds, drivers who substitute for Lee while he recuperates from gallbladder surgery. You might want to prepare a separate T-chart to contrast Lee with each substitute bus driver. The T-chart to contrast Lee and Thelma S. might look something like the one below.

After listing the differences between any two of the characters, introduce cue words that signal contrasts: *but, unlike, however, different, on the other hand, yet,* and *although*. Write these words on a chart or white erase board and refer to them while recapping the information on your T-chart. Begin by connecting each pair of phrases with the word *but*: *Lee gives out candy, but Thelma S. doesn't*. Then model how you could connect the contrasting ideas using the other cue words: *Although Lee gives out candy, Thelma S. doesn't. Lee knows the bus route; however, Thelma S. gets lost all the time.* Have students help construct the sentences.

For additional practice, have each student complete an organizer at his or her skill level.

Graphic Organizers

Beginning: **I Spy Some Differences**
(page 82)
Students contrast two characters or places in the book they are reading, draw pictures that show how they differ, and write a sentence describing one difference.

Lee	Thelma S.
Likes the Warren dogs	Bashes the dogs with her purse
Is a man	Is a woman
Gives out candy bars	Doesn't give candy
Plays a game	Doesn't play any games with the children
Knows the bus route	Gets lost all the time

Developing: **Digging for Differences**

(page 83)

Students contrast two characters, places, things, or events in a book they are reading and use a comparison chart to list differing characteristics.

Extending: **But They're Different**

(page 84)

Students contrast two characters, places, things, or events in a book they are reading, use a T-chart to list differing characteristics, and write a sentence telling how they differ. Students use a cue word in the sentence to signal the contrast.

Great Books for This Activity

Picture Books

Denslow, S. P. (1993). *Bus riders*. New York: Simon & Schuster.

Meddaugh, S. (1991). *The witches' supermarket*. New York: Houghton Mifflin.

Sendak, M. (1963). *Where the wild things are*. New York: Harper & Row. Contrast pictures as you move through the book, especially the first picture of Max's bedroom and the picture of his bedroom being transformed into a jungle.

Sturges, P. (1998). *Bridges are to cross*. New York: G.P. Putnam's Sons. Contrast the bridges in this book or focus just on the Tower Bridge, which contains two different bridges.

Chapter Book

Coerr, E. (1981). *The big balloon race*. New York: HarperCollins. Contrast how the mother and daughter felt at the beginning and end of the race.

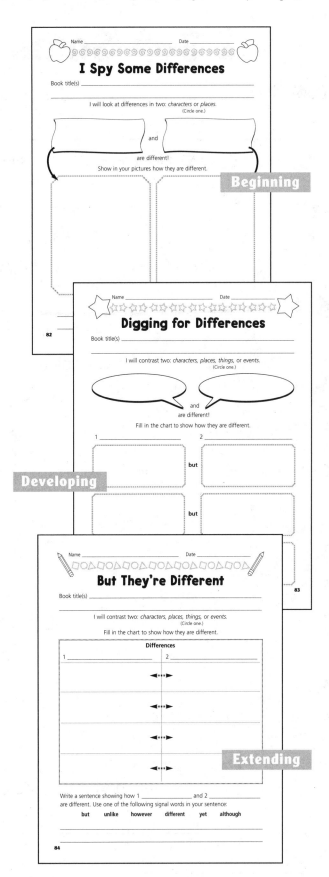

Name _____ Date _____

I Spy Some Differences

Book title(s) _____

_____

I will look at differences in two: *characters* or *places*.

(Circle one.)

and

are different!

Show in your pictures how they are different.

Tell about one difference in your pictures.

_____

_____

Digging for Differences

Book title(s) _____

_____

I will contrast two: *characters, places, things,* or *events.*

(Circle one.)

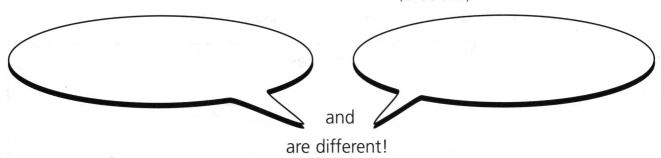

and

are different!

Fill in the chart to show how they are different.

1 _____   2 _____

	but	
	but	
	but	

But They're Different

Book title(s) _____

_____

I will contrast two: *characters, places, things,* or *events.*

(Circle one.)

Fill in the chart to show how they are different.

Differences	
1 _____	2 _____

Write a sentence showing how 1 _____ and 2 _____
are different. Use one of the following signal words in your sentence:

but   unlike   however   different   yet   although

_____

_____

Context Clues

Skill: *Determine the meaning of unfamiliar words by using the surrounding text.*

Description

Readers can often determine the meaning of an unfamiliar word by using information that precedes and follows it—in other words, by using context clues. This can be challenging for primary-grade readers for several reasons. First, to use context clues, readers need to recognize that words in a sentence, or paragraph, work together to influence the meaning of an unfamiliar word. Second, they need to be able to think critically—to draw conclusions and make logical connections between ideas. Finally, they need to be able to use sophisticated reading strategies, such as skipping an unfamiliar word momentarily—something primary-grade students may just be learning.

Although challenging, using context clues is an important comprehension skill that teachers can introduce incrementally at appropriate levels. Using context clues allows students to construct meaning from texts and to be independent readers.

Getting to Know the Concept

Introduce context clues by using books from the I Spy series (Marzollo and Wick) or the Where's Waldo series (Handford) that encourage students to use visual context clues, which are more concrete and accessible than textual clues. Allow students time to hunt for the hidden objects and then discuss the strategies they use to locate the objects. Perhaps they focus exclusively on searching for a specific color; or scan the picture one section at a time, looking globally for anything they can find; or perhaps they concentrate on finding a specific shape or pattern (Waldo's cane or his striped shirt).

Teaching the Concept With Literature

After students have had time to share their strategies, explain that when readers get stuck on unfamiliar words, they, too, use strategies to help them figure out the words. Compare what the students just did while searching for the hidden objects with what readers do when using context clues. In each case, the person hunts for information on the page that will be useful in helping him or her find an object or determine meaning. Using Big Books as you model context clues allows you to point out

important clues from illustrations and print. As you identify clues, explain how you are using them to determine the meaning of a targeted word.

Model Lesson

Begin by explaining that even the best readers don't always know every word on every page. When readers get stuck on a word, they can use information in the pictures and in sentences around the unfamiliar word to figure it out. Explain to students that you'll begin by using words they already know to practice this new skill.

Use a simple text and target a word students know. For instance, use *Whistle for Willie* (Keats, 1964) and read until you come to the word *drew* (unpaged). Explain that you are going to use as many clues as you can from the sentences that come before and after the word, from the pictures, and from decoding the word to learn about this word. Model your process. You might use the following steps: Read the page, skipping over this targeted word. Paraphrase what you read. Next, note what's going on in the picture and talk about the clues you got from it. Then write the target word on a white erase board, circling what you already know about the word (e.g., the beginning sound of *drew* is /dr/). Recap all you've found out about this word, read it, and explain what it means. Finally, reread the page to see if your definition makes sense.

You and your students will need to practice this strategy a number of times

with familiar words before moving on to unfamiliar words. Have students show what they used from the word, the text, and their own background to approximate a meaning.

For additional practice, have each student complete an organizer at his or her skill level.

Graphic Organizers

The Beginning and Developing graphic organizers are designed to help students understand and reinforce the process of locating context clues; therefore, you should identify familiar words for them to use in these activities. Students using the Extending graphic organizer should understand the process and be ready to apply it with an unfamiliar word.

Beginning: **Uncovering Context Clues** (page 88)
Students write the sentence containing the target word, draw pictures detailing what happened in the story just before and just after the target word, circle parts of the word they can decode, and write what they think the word means.

Developing: **Mystery Solved!** (page 89)
Students write the sentence containing the target word, draw pictures about what happened in the story just before and just after the target word, and tell what clues the pictures gave them about their word. They circle the parts of the word they can decode, and write what they think the word means.

Extending: **Sighting Signs** (page 90)
Students write a sentence containing an unfamiliar word, draw pictures or write about what happened in the story just before and just after the unfamiliar word. They think about what they know about the word so far, sound it out, define it, and use it in a new sentence.

Great Books for This Activity

Picture Books

Hautzig, D. (1984). *Little witch's big night.* New York: Random House. This easy reader will have both familiar words and some unfamiliar ones for students to investigate.

Keats, E. J. (1964). *Whistle for Willie.* New York: Scholastic.

McPhail, D. (1999). *Mole music.* New York: Henry Holt. The illustration and text enable students to use words, pictures, and their own experiences as context clues for easily decoded words such as *scale*, as well as challenging words such as *audience*.

Chapter Book

Davidson, M. (1964). *The story of Thomas Alva Edison, inventor: The wizard of Menlo Park.* New York: Scholastic. Pictures lend some support, but most of the context clues come from the text in this book.

Name _____ Date _____

Uncovering Context Clues

Book title _____

🔍 Your word: _____

📖 Write the sentence that has your word in it. _____

_____

Draw what happened in the story just **before** you found your word. | Draw what happened in the story just **after** you found your word.

Write your word. Use one box for each letter. Circle the letters you can sound out.

☐ ☐ ☐ ☐ ☐ ☐ ☐ ☐ ☐ ☐

What do you think your word means? _____

_____

Name _____ Date _____

Mystery Solved!

Book title _____

🔍 Your word: _____

📖 Write the sentence that has your word in it. _____

_____

Draw a picture of what happened in the story just **before** you found your word.

Draw a picture of what happened in the story just **after** you found your word.

What clues did your pictures give you about your word?

- _____

- _____

- _____

Write your word. Use one box for each letter. Circle the letters you can sound out.

☐ ☐ ☐ ☐ ☐ ☐ ☐ ☐ ☐

What do you think your word means? _____

_____

Name _____   Date _____

Sighting Signs

Book title _____

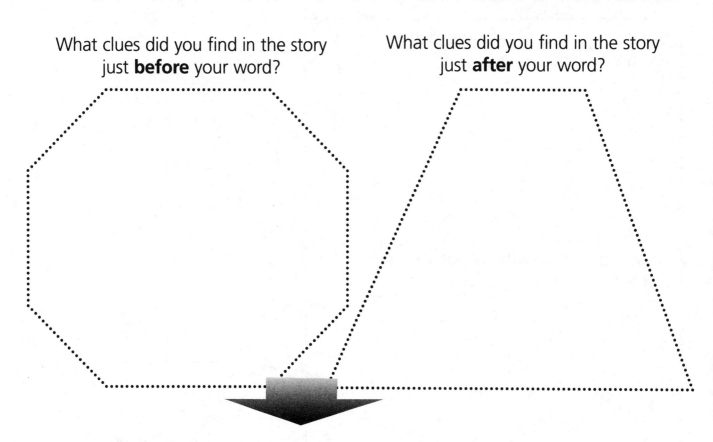

Your word: _____

Write the sentence that has your word in it. _____

_____

What clues did you find in the story just **before** your word?

What clues did you find in the story just **after** your word?

1. Think about what you already know about your word.

2. Sound out your word.

3. Write what you think your word means and use it in a new sentence.

My word means: _____

My new sentence: _____

_____

Summary

Skill: *Combine key points in a text to produce a concise synopsis.*

Description

Creating a summary can be challenging, even for older students, but we can introduce students to summarizing in the primary grades if we use developmentally appropriate language and activities. When we summarize, we determine the important information from a text and then use our own words to condense the ideas into a sentence or a few sentences. Summarization is an important comprehension skill. Since we can't remember all that we read, we need to hold on to the key points in the text. Good readers stop periodically and monitor what they are reading to be sure they are building an on-going inner account. When summarizing, we want young readers to think about the beginning, middle, and end of the story and then put the key ideas together into a shortened version that contains only the main points.

Getting to Know the Concept

We begin with oral summaries that are based on familiar experiences. For example, you might think aloud about what you did to get ready for school and list the information on a chart. You might have items such as brushed my teeth, washed my face and hands, went to the kitchen, filled a bowl with cereal and fruit, sat down, ate breakfast, put on my socks, pants, belt, top, and shoes. Reread your list and talk about whether or not you need all these details to help someone else know about the early part of your day. Suggest that some of the small details could be grouped together and relabeled. Circle the first two items on your list, for example, and explain that you could say you "washed up." Circle the next four items and write "had breakfast" beside them. Circle the last five items and write "got dressed" beside them. Read just the labels: I washed up, had breakfast, and got dressed. Continue to model this process, perhaps detailing how you got from your home to school.

Take advantage of what you and your students are doing throughout the day to model summarization. You can recap the key steps you use to clean the gerbil cage or recall major events at recess or when you transition from circle time. Provide a summary for each activity and gradually have students take on some of the responsibility for creating these oral summaries. To help students determine the important ideas and combine smaller details into a broader idea, you might give support by saying, "First . . . Then . . . After that . . . Finally . . ."

Teaching the Concept With Literature

Once your students have had some practice summarizing their personal experiences, it's time to introduce summarization with literature. Again, since summarization is a challenging concept, use familiar texts so students can focus all their attention on the comprehension task.

Begin by reading aloud books with simple story lines, such as *Dear Zoo* (Campbell, 1982). Talk about the following:

❋ The main character and what happened at the beginning of the story

❋ What happened in the middle of the story

❋ How the story ended

Use these same basic points consistently to practice summarization.

Model Lesson

Whistle for Willie (Keats, 1964) is a beloved picture book about Peter, a little boy who wants desperately to learn how to whistle. If you have a Big-Book version of this story, use it for this lesson. To begin, on chart paper draw a three-box chart, similar to Picture a Story, the beginning-level graphic organizer (page 94). After reading *Whistle for Willie* to the class, model how you would complete this chart, drawing a picture for each box. Once complete, review what you drew to be sure it is an accurate synopsis of the story. Next, beside or under each picture, write what the picture is about. Reread what you wrote and explain that you have a one-minute story—a summary of the

original *Whistle for Willie*.

When students are ready to try summarizing with longer texts, model with the first chapter from an easy chapter book, such as *Owl at Home* (Lobel, 1975). This time, write out short phrases for the events that happened at the beginning, the middle, and the end of the story. Finally, reread the summary, inserting transition words (*at first, then, after that, finally*) where they belong and read the summary again. Modeling this process will help students realize that they should include in their summaries important events—but not every detail associated with each event.

For additional practice, have each student complete an organizer at his or her skill level.

Graphic Organizers

Beginning: **Picture a Story** (page 94)
Students draw three pictures: one showing who the story is about and what happened in the beginning of the story; one showing something important that happened in the middle of the story; and one showing how the story ended. Students use the organizer to provide an oral summary of the story.

Developing: **Sum It Up!** (page 95)
Students write the main character's name and what happened at the beginning of the story. Next, students draw two pictures showing important events that happened in the middle of the story. Students write how the story ended. Students use the organizer to provide an oral or written summary of the story.

Extending: **One-Minute Story** (page 96)
Students name the character in the story and write what happened at the beginning, in the middle, and at the end of the story. They use transition words and reread what they have written, to be sure they have an accurate summary of the story.

Great Books for This Activity

Picture Books

Campbell, R. (1982). *Dear zoo.* New York: Trumpet Club.

Cooney, B. (1982). *Miss Rumphius.* New York: Viking.

Keats, E. J. (1964). *Whistle for Willie.* New York: Scholastic.

Lobel, A. (1975). *Owl at home.* New York: Harper & Row.

West, C. (1986). *"Pardon?" said the giraffe.* New York: Trophy.

Picture Book

Adler, D. A. (1982). *Cam Jansen and the mystery of the Babe Ruth baseball.* New York: Puffin.

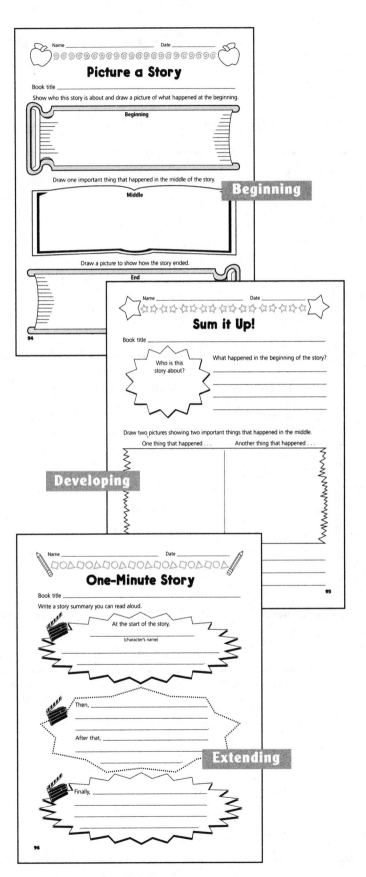

Name _____ Date _____

Picture a Story

Book title _____

Show who this story is about and draw a picture of what happened at the beginning.

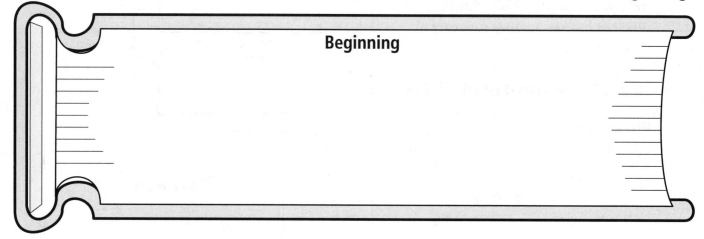

Beginning

Draw one important thing that happened in the middle of the story.

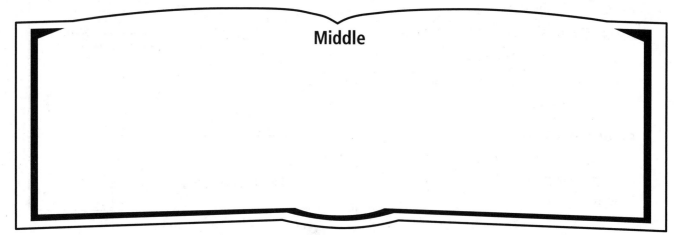

Middle

Draw a picture to show how the story ended.

End

Name ______________________ Date ______________

Sum it Up!

Book title ____

Who is this story about?

What happened in the beginning of the story?

____

____

____

____

Draw two pictures showing two important things that happened in the middle.

One thing that happened . . .

Another thing that happened . . .

How did the story end? ____

____

____

One-Minute Story

Book title _____

Write a story summary you can read aloud.

At the start of the story,

_____
(character's name)

_____

_____ .

Then, _____

_____

_____ .

After that, _____

_____

_____ .

Finally, _____

_____

_____

_____ .